ABIDE

Living and Remaining in the Love of Christ

A 100-Day Devotional on Intimacy, Surrender, and Transformation

Ruth Conlon

Eternal *life*
Publishers

EternalLife Publishers is a publishing ministry with a passion for spiritual development. We produce individual and group resources to accompany you on your sacred journey. For more information on our training and products, go to www.pursuingholiness.org. EternalLife Publishers is the publishing arm of Pursuing Holiness Ministries.

Email: info@pursuingholiness.org

Published by EternalLife Publishers, a part of Pursuing Holiness Ministries

London, England

www.pursuingholiness.org

Book Layout by EternalLife Publishers

Cover designed by EternalLife Publishers

Abide / Ruth Conlon. —1st Ed.

ISBN 978-1-0684743-0-9

Table of Contents

Introduction

To abide is to remain, to rest, to live in continuous communion with Christ. This devotional is not just an invitation to linger near Jesus, but to live rooted in Him. In a world constantly tugging us toward performance, distraction, and striving, abiding is an act of spiritual resistance. It is the daily choice to centre our hearts, minds, and entire being around the presence of God.

Through these one hundred devotionals, we will explore what it means to truly live and remain in the love of Christ. Each day is designed to deepen your spiritual formation through scripture, reflection, personal affirmation, and daily practice. Quotes from mystics, saints, and modern-day voices will help guide your journey.

This is not a journey of perfection, but of presence. May your soul be stilled, your roots go deep, and your love for God grow ever more abiding.

1

Abiding Begins with Belovedness

"We are not what we do. We are not what we have. We are not what others say about us. We are the beloved daughters and sons of God." — Henri Nouwen

Scripture Meditation

"As the Father has loved me, so have I loved you. Now remain in my love." — John 15:9 (NIV)

Before abiding becomes a practice, it is first a position. You begin not with action, but identity. Jesus says, "Remain in my love," because love is the soil where abiding grows.

Many try to abide without first receiving this truth: you are deeply, irrevocably, eternally loved. To abide without belovedness is to strive. To abide *in* belovedness is to rest.

God doesn't ask you to prove your worth—He invites you to remain in the worth He has already spoken over you. Abiding starts with saying yes to being loved.

Personal Affirmation

I am the beloved of God. His love is my home, my foundation, and my true identity.

Reflection Questions

- Do you find it easier to do for God than to be loved by God?
- How would your spiritual life change if you truly believed you are beloved?

Practice for Today

Sit still for five minutes. As you breathe in, whisper, 'I am loved.' As you breathe out, whisper, 'I remain in Your love.'

Prayer

Father, help me receive the truth that I am Your beloved. Let Your love be more than a concept—let it be my constant dwelling. Amen.

2

Learning to Remain

"Remaining is not about standing still. It is about staying connected while moving forward." — Ruth Haley Barton

Scripture Meditation

"Remain in me, as I also remain in you." — John 15:4 (NIV)

To remain is to stay with, to cling to, to not wander off. It's a holy kind of stubbornness—the kind that holds on when everything else says let go.

Abiding doesn't always look spiritual. Sometimes it looks like choosing stillness in a storm. Sometimes it's refusing to numb the ache. Sometimes it's whispering, 'Jesus, I trust You' when nothing makes sense.

Remaining isn't passive—it's an active devotion. A moment-by-moment return. A rhythm of choosing Him again, and again, and again.

Personal Affirmation

I am learning to remain. Even in uncertainty, I choose to stay rooted in Christ.

Reflection Questions

- When are you most tempted to drift from God?
- What does remaining in Christ look like in your daily routine?

Practice for Today

Set a timer for midday. When it rings, pause, breathe, and pray: 'Jesus, I choose to remain in You.'

Prayer

Jesus, teach me to remain. When I am restless, draw me back. When I drift, hold me fast. Abide in me as I abide in You. Amen.

3

The Slow Work of God

"Above all, trust in the slow work of God." — Pierre Teilhard de Chardin

Scripture Meditation

"He has made everything beautiful in its time." — Ecclesiastes 3:11 (NIV)

Abiding requires patience. It is the surrender of our timelines for the beauty of God's timing. In the slow work, roots go deep. In the waiting, trust is formed.

We often want spiritual growth to be instant, visible, impressive. But God prefers cultivation to speed. His work is thorough, hidden, and enduring.

To abide is to believe that what God is doing in you—though slow—is sacred. There is no rush in the rhythms of the Vine.

Personal Affirmation

I trust the slow work of God. His timing is perfect, and His process is wise.

Reflection Questions

- Where do you feel tempted to rush God?
- How can you cultivate trust in His perfect pace today?

Practice for Today

Take a short walk at half your usual speed. Let each step be a prayer of surrender to God's pace.

Prayer

Lord, I trust You with time. Grow me deep, not fast. Let my life move to the rhythm of Your grace. Amen.

4

Fruit Comes from Union

"The branch does not produce fruit by effort, but by abiding." — Andrew Murray

Scripture Meditation

"No branch can bear fruit by itself; it must remain in the vine." — John 15:4 (NIV)

In the kingdom of God, fruit is not manufactured—it is borne. It doesn't come from striving, but from staying. The life of the Vine flows into the branch, and the result is fruit.

Abiding keeps you close enough for that flow to continue. When you are united with Christ—when you dwell, listen, surrender—the fruit of His Spirit begins to appear: love, joy, peace, patience...

You don't grow these by force. You grow them by union.

Personal Affirmation

I am connected to the Vine. My life will bear fruit through union, not effort.

Reflection Questions

- In what ways are you trying to force spiritual fruit?
- How can you stay more deeply connected to Jesus today?

Practice for Today

Choose one fruit of the Spirit and reflect on it for five minutes. Ask God to grow it in you—not by effort, but by grace.

Prayer

Jesus, I don't want to fake fruit. I want to bear it through You. Help me stay so close that Your life becomes mine. Amen.

5

When Nothing Seems to Grow

"Do not seek to measure the fruit. Seek only to remain rooted." — Thomas Merton

Scripture Meditation:

"Let us not become weary in doing good, for at the proper time we will reap a harvest if we do not give up." — Galatians 6:9 (NIV)

Some seasons feel barren. You remain, you pray, you serve—and yet, nothing seems to bloom. In these times, trust this truth: fruit is often forming where eyes cannot see.

The hidden work of abiding is not wasted. Roots grow before fruit appears. What feels like stillness may be deepening. What feels like delay may be preparation.

Abide anyway. Not because you see results, but because He is worthy. God honors the faithful soul who stays even when it feels unseen.

Personal Affirmation

Even when I see no fruit, I trust God is working. My roots are growing deeper in Him.

Reflection Questions

- Are you discouraged by what seems like spiritual dryness?
- What helps you keep abiding even when growth isn't visible?

Practice for Today

Spend time in prayer today without asking for anything. Just be with God. Let your presence be your offering.

Prayer

God, when I cannot see the fruit, help me trust the roots. Grow me deeper. Keep me near. I choose to abide in faith. Amen.

6

The Abiding Life Is a Listening Life

"The closer you get to God, the more real His whispers become." — Teresa of Ávila

Scripture Meditation

"My sheep listen to my voice; I know them, and they follow me." — John 10:27 (NIV)

Abiding is not only about speaking to God—it's about listening. Not for thunderclaps or divine commands, but for the gentle nudges and sacred stillness that often come without sound.

The abiding soul becomes attuned to the whisper. It listens with expectancy. It leans in when the world shouts.

Hearing God doesn't require volume—it requires closeness. And abiding is the way we draw close enough to hear the quiet voice that shapes everything.

Personal Affirmation

I hear the voice of God. I am His sheep, and I know His whisper.

Reflection Questions

- What helps you tune into God's voice?
- Are there distractions you need to silence to hear Him more clearly?

Practice for Today

Take five minutes in silence. Begin with this prayer: 'Speak, Lord. Your servant is listening.' Then wait. Just wait.

Prayer

God of the whisper, tune my ears to Your voice. Let me not miss You in the noise. Let my heart learn to listen in love. Amen.

7

Remaining Through Resistance

"When the soul holds fast to God, even resistance becomes an altar." — Catherine of Siena

Scripture Meditation

"Blessed is the one who perseveres under trial because, having stood the test, that person will receive the crown of life." — James 1:12 (NIV)

Sometimes abiding means staying when everything in you wants to flee. Resistance isn't always external—often, it's internal. Doubt, fear, weariness—they all pull at your resolve.

But every moment you choose to remain, to lean in instead of run, you are being formed. You're offering your presence as a sacrifice of trust.

Even resistance can become worship when it leads you to depend more deeply on Jesus. Abiding isn't about having no struggle—it's about clinging to Christ in the midst of it.

Personal Affirmation

I remain in Christ even through resistance. His grace sustains me when I feel weak.

Reflection Questions

- Where are you experiencing resistance in your spiritual walk?
- What would it look like to remain even now?

Practice for Today

Name one area of resistance. Write it down, then lay your hand over it and pray: 'God, help me remain here with You.'

Prayer

Jesus, I want to stay close—even when it's hard. Strengthen me. Remind me that every resistance is an invitation to depend on You more. Amen.

8

The Joy of Attachment

"Joy is the infallible sign of the presence of God." — Pierre
Teilhard de Chardin

Scripture Meditation

"I have told you this so that my joy may be in you and that your joy
may be complete." — John 15:11 (NIV)

Abiding isn't a life of heaviness—it is a life of joy. Jesus connects joy
directly to remaining in Him. Joy is not found in independence, but
in attachment.

We often try to create joy through experiences or achievements, but
true joy flows from union with Christ. It's not the result of perfect
circumstances, but of perfect connection.

When you abide, joy becomes your inheritance—not a temporary
feeling, but a steady river flowing from the heart of God into yours.

Personal Affirmation

I am joined to the Vine, and His joy flows through me. My joy is
rooted in His presence.

Reflection Questions

- What has been your usual source of joy?
- How does abiding shift your understanding of lasting joy?

Practice for Today

Reflect on a recent moment of joy. Trace it back to God's presence. Thank Him, and ask for deeper awareness of joy in your abiding.

Prayer

Jesus, thank You that joy is found in You. Let my joy be full, not from fleeting things, but from deep connection with You. Amen.

9

Withness Before Witness

"We must first be with Him before we can be sent by Him."
— Dallas Willard

Scripture Meditation

"He appointed twelve that they might be with him and that he might send them out." — Mark 3:14 (NIV)

In the world of ministry and mission, it's easy to run without resting, to speak without listening, to do without being. But Jesus' first call to His disciples was not to preach—it was to *be with Him*.

Abiding is about *withness*. Before we can represent Christ, we must remain with Christ. It's the closeness that gives power to the message, intimacy that births authority.

Don't be in a rush to witness without withness. Abiding ensures your life speaks what your lips declare.

Personal Affirmation

I abide before I act. I stay with Jesus before I speak for Jesus.

Reflection Questions

- Have you been prioritising doing for God over being with God?
- How can you re-centre your life around withness today?

Practice for Today

Before any major task or conversation today, pause for one minute and say, 'Jesus, I want to be with You before I move for You.'

Prayer

Jesus, let my witness flow from withness. Teach me to stay before I go, to be before I speak. Dwell with me, and shape me. Amen.

10

The Vine Never Leaves

"Even when we let go, grace holds fast." — Brennan Manning

Scripture Meditation

"And surely I am with you always, to the very end of the age." — Matthew 28:20 (NIV)

Abiding isn't only about your grip on God—it's about His grip on you. The Vine never detaches. Even when you feel weak, distracted, or distant, He remains.

The enemy would love to convince you that your failures or forgetfulness have severed the connection. But the truth is, the Vine is faithful. He holds what you can't.

Abiding is less about striving and more about surrender. You are held. You are kept. You are still connected.

Personal Affirmation

Even in my weakness, God holds me. The Vine never lets go.

Reflection Questions

- Do you ever feel like you've fallen too far from God to return?
- What does it mean to you that Jesus is always with you?

Practice for Today

Spend one minute with your hands open on your lap. Pray this: 'Jesus, thank You for holding me when I cannot hold You.'

Prayer

Faithful Vine, thank You that You never leave. Even when I waver, You are near. Let me rest in Your unshakeable presence. Amen.

11

Abiding Through Disappointment

"God does not waste your pain. He uses it to draw you deeper into His presence." — Elisabeth Elliot

Scripture Meditation

"The Lord is close to the brokenhearted and saves those who are crushed in spirit." — Psalm 34:18 (NIV)

Disappointment often tempts us to retreat. When life doesn't turn out as hoped, abiding feels harder—but it's also more necessary.

Jesus invites us not to deny disappointment, but to bring it to Him. To remain even when the road winds through questions and unmet desires. This is not weak faith—it's faithful surrender.

Abiding through disappointment doesn't mean pretending to be okay. It means trusting that even here, especially here, you are not alone.

Personal Affirmation

I can abide even in disappointment. God is with me in my sorrow, and He is faithful to restore.

Reflection Questions

- What recent disappointment has challenged your ability to remain in Christ?

- How might God be meeting you even in what feels broken?

Practice for Today

Name your disappointment to God aloud in prayer. Then sit for five minutes, inviting Him to draw near to you there.

Prayer

Jesus, meet me in my sorrow. I bring You the places that ache. Help me to abide, not just in joy, but in grief. Draw near and hold me close. Amen.

12

The Strength of Stillness

"It is in stillness that the soul most deeply knows God." — Thomas Keating

Scripture Meditation

"In repentance and rest is your salvation, in quietness and trust is your strength." — Isaiah 30:15 (NIV)

In a culture of motion and noise, stillness can feel like weakness. But in God's economy, it's strength. The quiet soul is not passive—it is rooted.

Abiding calls you into rhythms of silence and solitude, not to escape the world but to re-centre in the One who holds it. Strength comes not from pushing through, but from leaning in.

Stillness trains your heart to listen, to notice, to breathe. And in the quiet, God restores what busyness tries to bury.

Personal Affirmation

Stillness is not empty. It is full of God. I receive strength in quiet trust.

Reflection Questions

- How comfortable are you with stillness in your walk with God?
- What fears or distractions might stillness be inviting you to surrender?

Practice for Today

Set a timer for ten minutes. Sit in complete stillness. Breathe slowly and repeat: 'In quietness and trust is my strength.'

Prayer

God of peace, draw me into stillness. Let me rest in You and receive strength not from doing, but from abiding. Amen.

13

Rooted in the Word

"To abide in His Word is to let it dwell in you richly, shaping your thoughts, your longings, your very life." — Dietrich Bonhoeffer

Scripture Meditation

"If you remain in me and my words remain in you, ask whatever you wish, and it will be done for you." — John 15:7 (NIV)

Abiding is not just emotional—it's scriptural. Jesus ties remaining in Him to remaining in His words. The Word of God is not a textbook; it's the breath of the Vine, flowing into the branches.

To abide in the Word means letting it shape your daily rhythm. Not just reading it, but meditating on it, responding to it, allowing it to change you from within.

You cannot remain in Jesus and neglect His words. His voice and presence go hand in hand.

Personal Affirmation

The Word of God lives in me. I am shaped, rooted, and nourished by His truth.

Reflection Questions

- What does it mean for God's Word to 'remain in you'?
- How can you let Scripture speak into your inner world today?

Practice for Today

Choose one verse from John 15. Write it on a notecard or note app. Reflect on it throughout your day, letting it guide your thoughts.

Prayer

Living Word, dwell in me. Let Your truth remain in my heart, renew my mind, and guide my steps. I choose to abide in Your Word today. Amen.

14

Returning Again and Again

"The spiritual life is simply returning to God over and over again, and never being shamed away." — Henri Nouwen

Scripture Meditation

"Return to me, for I have redeemed you." — Isaiah 44:22 (NIV)

Abiding doesn't mean you never drift. It means you keep returning. The abiding life is one of continual renewal, where coming back is part of the rhythm.

The enemy wants to use your failures to keep you distant. But God uses them as bridges back to closeness. Every return is an act of grace. Every moment of reconnection is a miracle.

There is no shame in coming back. Jesus is not weary of your return— He's waiting for it.

Personal Affirmation

I return to God again and again. His grace welcomes me without shame.

Reflection Questions

- Have you been avoiding God because of guilt or failure?

- What would it look like to return fully today?

Practice for Today

Write a short prayer of return. It doesn't need to be perfect—just real. Offer it to God as an act of abiding.

Prayer

Jesus, I return again. Not with fear, but with hope. You are always here. Let me remain where love never runs out. Amen.

15

Closeness Over Clarity

"We want clarity, but God invites us to trust. Clarity is a gift; trust is a choice." — Corrie ten Boom

Scripture Meditation

"Trust in the Lord with all your heart and lean not on your own understanding." — Proverbs 3:5 (NIV)

We often want answers more than presence. We want God to explain everything, to draw a map before we take the next step. But abiding doesn't promise clarity—it offers closeness.

When we remain in Christ, we may not always know *why*, but we always know *who* is with us. Trust becomes our anchor when understanding runs thin. The abiding soul learns to prefer nearness to certainty.

Let your peace come not from having all the answers, but from staying close to the One who does.

Personal Affirmation

I choose trust over clarity. Closeness with Christ is enough for me.

Reflection Questions

- Are you waiting on clarity before choosing to abide?
- How might trust be calling you deeper into relationship today?

Practice for Today

Name an area where you feel unclear. Say aloud: 'I don't understand, but I choose to trust You here.'

Prayer

God, I want answers, but I need You more. Teach me to abide in trust. Let Your presence be the peace I long for. Amen.

16

The Rest of Abiding

"We rest because God is at work. We cease striving to let Him be our strength." — Eugene Peterson

Scripture Meditation:

"Come to me, all you who are weary and burdened, and I will give you rest." — Matthew 11:28 (NIV)

Abiding is not just an activity—it is a posture of rest. In a world that glorifies hustle and hurry, the soul that abides becomes a witness to divine rest.

Jesus does not demand you carry everything. He invites you to come to Him, to unburden, to breathe. Rest is not weakness—it is trust in the God who works even when you pause.

Rest is worship. When you cease striving and choose stillness, you declare, 'God, I trust You more than my effort.'

Personal Affirmation

I am not driven—I am drawn. I rest because God is working in me and for me.

Reflection Questions

- Where is your soul weary today?
- What might you need to release in order to rest more deeply?

Practice for Today

Take a nap, a walk, or a moment of pause—not as an escape, but as worship. Let your rest say, 'God is enough.'

Prayer

Jesus, I come weary. I lay down my burdens. Teach me the rhythm of Your rest. Let abiding restore what hurry has drained. Amen.

17

Pruned to Bear More

"God prunes us when He is about to take us into a new season of fruitfulness." — Oswald Chambers

Scripture Meditation

"He cuts off every branch in me that bears no fruit, while every branch that does bear fruit he prunes so that it will be even more fruitful." — John 15:2 (NIV)

Abiding doesn't mean you'll never experience pain. Sometimes it includes pruning—divine cutting away of what hinders growth. But it is not punishment—it is preparation.

God prunes not because you are failing, but because you are fruitful. The branches that show promise are the ones He shapes most attentively.

Trust the pruning. It is proof of your connectedness. It is love with shears, tending you toward your fullest potential in Christ.

Personal Affirmation

I trust the pruning of God. He is making space for more fruit in me.

Reflection Questions

- What might God be lovingly cutting away in this season?
- How can you respond to pruning with surrender instead of resistance?

Practice for Today

Journal a list of things God may be pruning in you. Offer each one in prayer, trusting His hand in the process.

Prayer

Master Gardener, I surrender to Your pruning. Though it may sting, I trust Your vision. Make me more fruitful by Your grace. Amen.

18

Abiding Through Silence

"Silence is God's first language. Everything else is a poor translation." — Thomas Keating

Scripture Meditation

"The LORD is in his holy temple; let all the earth be silent before him." — Habakkuk 2:20 (NIV)

There are seasons when God feels silent—not absent, but quiet. In those moments, abiding invites us not to panic, but to lean in.

The silence of God is not always a void. Sometimes, it's an invitation into deeper listening. An unveiling of presence that doesn't need to speak to be real.

To abide through silence is to remain when answers don't come quickly. It is faith that trusts God is near, even when He whispers nothing at all.

Personal Affirmation

Even in the silence, I remain. God is with me, and I am not alone.

Reflection Questions

- When have you experienced the silence of God?
- How might silence be forming something sacred in you?

Practice for Today

Spend five minutes in complete silence before God. Instead of asking for anything, simply say: 'Here I am.'

Prayer

God of the quiet, teach me to trust You in silence. Let stillness shape my soul and deepen my abiding. Amen.

19

Letting the Vine Define You

"Your identity is not in your branch, but in your connection to the Vine." — Brennan Manning

Scripture Meditation

"You did not choose me, but I chose you and appointed you so that you might go and bear fruit." — John 15:16 (NIV)

So much of life tells us we are what we do, how we look, or what we've achieved. But Jesus redefines us. In Him, we are chosen, appointed, and connected.

Abiding means letting God name you. It means letting go of false identities and holding onto the truth that your worth flows from the Vine.

You don't have to prove yourself. You are already His. Let that identity ground you today.

Personal Affirmation

I am chosen by God. My identity is rooted in Him, not in what I do.

Reflection Questions

- Where do you often find your identity apart from Christ?
- What changes when you remember that God chose you first?

Practice for Today

Write the words: 'I am chosen, appointed, and loved.' Repeat them throughout your day whenever you feel uncertain.

Prayer

Jesus, thank You for choosing me. Help me let go of every false identity and root myself in You alone. Amen.

20

The Secret of Staying

"The greatest act of spiritual warfare is to stay where God has planted you." — Watchman Nee

Scripture Meditation

"Those who remain in me, and I in them, will produce much fruit."
—John 15:5 (NLT)

Sometimes the holiest thing you can do is stay. Not run. Not start over. Just stay—rooted, trusting, growing.

Abiding doesn't promise ease. In fact, it often calls for perseverance. The vine doesn't uproot itself in storm or drought—it digs deeper.

The secret to spiritual vitality is not constant movement, but holy staying. In abiding, you discover that God is not only in the fruit—but also in the faithfulness.

Personal Affirmation

I choose to stay where God has planted me. Abiding is my strength and my shield.

Reflection Questions

* What area of your life feels difficult to remain in right now?
* How can staying become a spiritual offering today?

Practice for Today

Say aloud, 'I will stay.' Let it be a declaration of faith in God's timing, presence, and fruitfulness.

Prayer

Father, help me remain when I feel like running. Teach me the beauty of staying rooted in You. Let faithfulness be my worship. Amen.

21

The Flow of the Vine

"As we abide, His life flows through ours — unnoticed, yet undeniable." — Madame Guyon

Scripture Meditation

"I am the vine; you are the branches. If you remain in me and I in you, you will bear much fruit." — John 15:5 (NIV)

The power of the abiding life is not in what you force—it's in what flows. Like sap in a vine, Christ's life enters yours through consistent connection.

You don't need to manufacture fruit. You need only stay connected. When you remain in Him, what flows from Him—peace, love, truth—flows into you.

Abiding is trusting the flow. The Spirit works silently, steadily, shaping you in ways unseen but eternal.

Personal Affirmation

Christ's life flows through me. I am a vessel of His presence, power, and peace.

Reflection Questions

- Are you trusting God's flow or trying to force results?
- Where do you sense the Spirit's quiet work in you today?

Practice for Today

Close your eyes and breathe deeply for two minutes. Imagine the life of Christ flowing into you. Whisper: 'I receive Your life.'

Prayer

Jesus, let Your Spirit flow freely through me. May I stay close enough to feel Your presence and bear fruit that reflects Your heart. Amen.

22

Dwell, Don't Visit

"God doesn't want weekend guests. He desires full-time residents." — Brother Lawrence

Scripture Meditation

"Whoever dwells in the shelter of the Most High will rest in the shadow of the Almighty." — Psalm 91:1 (NIV)

To dwell is to live, not merely to stop by. Many approach God like a visitor—coming for help, encouragement, or inspiration—but then leaving again.

Abiding invites you to make your home in Him. Not occasionally, but daily. Constantly. To wake with Him, walk with Him, and rest with Him.

God wants habitation, not visitation. He doesn't just want moments with you—He wants all of you. Make Him your dwelling place.

Personal Affirmation

God is my home. I dwell, not visit. I remain, not rush.

Reflection Questions

- Are there areas of your life where God feels like a visitor rather than Lord?
- What does it mean for you to dwell with God in every part of your day?

Practice for Today

Take a walk and speak aloud, 'God, this moment is Yours. I dwell in You here.' Repeat it in different parts of your day.

Prayer

Lord, I don't want to just visit You—I want to live in You. Let my heart be rooted in Your presence all day, every day. Amen.

23

Fruit in Its Season

"The tree doesn't rush. It grows slowly and yields fruit in its time." — Saint John of the Cross

Scripture Meditation

"They are like a tree planted by streams of water, which yields its fruit in season." — Psalm 1:3 (NIV)

Abiding doesn't guarantee instant results. It promises fruit—in season. Like trees, your life is marked by rhythms: planting, waiting, growing, and finally, harvest.

Impatience will tempt you to uproot too soon. But abiding reminds you that timing belongs to God. Trust the slow miracle of becoming.

God is never late. Your fruit is coming—in its time. Stay rooted, watered by His presence, and watch what blooms.

Personal Affirmation

I trust God's timing. My life will bear fruit in its appointed season.

Reflection Questions

- Are you anxious about seeing results or fruit?
- How can you deepen your trust in God's perfect timing?

Practice for Today

Stand near a tree or plant. Reflect on how long it took to grow. Say: 'Lord, let me grow like this—deep, steady, and in season.'

Prayer

Lord of every season, help me not to rush the process. I trust that fruit will come as I abide in You. Keep me faithful. Amen.

24

Remaining in Love

"To abide in love is to keep choosing love, again and again, even when it costs." — Julian of Norwich

Scripture Meditation

"Now remain in my love." — John 15:9 (NIV)

The call to abide is, at its core, a call to remain in love—not just to know you are loved by God, but to live from that love, to act in it, and to extend it.

Love is not a fleeting feeling—it is a staying force. It anchors us when faith feels thin and hope feels distant. It is love that keeps us rooted when nothing else makes sense.

Remaining in love is choosing to see yourself and others through God's eyes. It's remaining open, soft, and surrendered to the One who is Love.

Personal Affirmation

I remain in God's love. His love surrounds, sustains, and transforms me.

Reflection Questions

- What does it mean for you to remain in love today?
- Who might need the overflow of that love through you?

Practice for Today

Write down three ways you've experienced God's love recently. Let gratitude grow your ability to remain in that love.

Prayer

Lord of love, I choose to remain. Help me abide not just in theory, but in action. Let me live and love from Your heart. Amen.

25

Steady in the Storm

"The storm reveals what the roots have been holding onto."
— St. Augustine

Scripture Meditation

"Then they cried out to the Lord in their trouble, and he brought them out of their distress. He stilled the storm to a whisper." — Psalm 107:28–29 (NIV)

Abiding doesn't prevent storms. It prepares you to remain rooted when they come. The winds may howl, the waters may rise, but the branch that stays connected to the Vine does not break.

In seasons of shaking, it is the depth of your attachment to Christ that holds you steady. He is not outside the storm—He is with you in it, anchoring your soul.

Abiding gives you resilience. It steadies your heart. It is the assurance that no matter what surrounds you, you are still held.

Personal Affirmation

I remain in Christ through every storm. He is my anchor and my calm.

Reflection Questions

- What storm are you walking through right now?
- How is God inviting you to trust and remain, even in chaos?

Practice for Today

Take time today to reflect on one past storm. Remember how God met you there. Let that memory anchor your current faith.

Prayer

God of peace, steady me when life shakes. Let me cling to You, trusting You are not only present—but powerful in the storm. Amen.

26

The Grace of Slowness

"Slowness is not God's absence. It is often His signature."
— John Ortberg

Scripture Meditation

"The Lord is not slow in keeping his promise, as some understand slowness. Instead he is patient with you." — 2 Peter 3:9 (NIV)

In a world racing for results, God walks at the pace of love. He moves slowly—not out of delay, but out of intention. The slow work of God is deep, steady, and lasting.

Abiding teaches us to move at the pace of grace. Not to rush spiritual growth or force breakthrough, but to let the Spirit form us slowly, layer by layer.

What feels slow is not wasted. It's holy. It's the process that produces fruit that lasts.

Personal Affirmation

I embrace the grace of slowness. God's timing is kind, and His pace is peace.

Reflection Questions

- Where are you tempted to rush what God is doing?
- How is God inviting you to slow down and stay close?

Practice for Today

Intentionally do something slowly today—a walk, a meal, a conversation. Let the pace remind you of God's gentleness.

Prayer

Patient Father, thank You for not rushing me. Help me slow down and align with Your pace. Let me be shaped by grace, not speed. Amen.

27

Intimacy Over Impact

"The goal is not to be impressive to the world but intimate with God." — A.W. Tozer

Scripture Meditation

"What good will it be for someone to gain the whole world, yet forfeit their soul?" — Matthew 16:26 (NIV)

Abiding confronts the need to prove, perform, and be seen. The world measures success by visibility. But God treasures intimacy.

It's possible to do great things and miss the One who called you. It's possible to touch many lives and lose your own soul in the process.

Abiding calls you back to the centre—where it's not about applause, but presence. Not about doing for God, but being with Him. Intimacy is the greater impact.

Personal Affirmation

I choose intimacy over impact. I am most fruitful when I am most connected to God.

Reflection Questions

- Where do you feel pressure to produce or prove?
- How might intimacy with God realign your priorities?

(ins

RUTH CONLON

Practice for Today

Cancel or pause one non-essential task today. Use that time to simply sit with God, with no agenda but to enjoy His presence.

Prayer

Jesus, I lay down the need to perform. Let me abide in Your love and choose closeness over being impressive. You are enough. Amen.

55

28

Daily Dependence

"God designed us to need Him every single day—not just in crisis, but in consistency." — Dallas Willard

Scripture Meditation:

"Give us today our daily bread." — Matthew 6:11 (NIV)

Abiding is not a once-a-week rhythm or a spiritual high. It's a daily dependence, a returning again and again to the Source of life.

God doesn't give grace for a year in advance—He gives daily bread. Enough for now. Abiding teaches us to ask, receive, and trust day by day.

Your need is not a flaw—it's your invitation. Dependence isn't weakness; it's the gateway to intimacy. The more you need Him, the closer you stay.

Personal Affirmation

I depend on God daily. His grace is my portion, and His presence is my strength.

Reflection Questions

- In what areas are you trying to live independently from God?
- What does daily dependence on Jesus look like for you today?

Practice for Today

Begin your day by praying: 'Jesus, I need You today. Give me what I cannot provide for myself. Help me stay close.'

Prayer

Father, thank You that I don't need to have it all figured out. Teach me to live in daily dependence and abide in Your endless supply. Amen.

29

Chosen to Stay Close

"You were not only saved from something; you were saved for someone — Jesus." — Henri Nouwen

Scripture Meditation

"You did not choose me, but I chose you and appointed you so that you might go and bear fruit." — John 15:16 (NIV)

Abiding begins not with your pursuit of God, but His pursuit of you. Jesus reminds us that He did the choosing. He initiated the connection. Your job is simply to stay close.

You were not chosen to strive, but to stay. Not selected to perform, but to be with Him. From this place of intimacy, the fruit comes naturally.

Let today be a reminder: you are already wanted. You don't need to earn belonging—you were handpicked to remain.

Personal Affirmation

I am chosen to stay close. My place with Jesus is secure and sure.

Reflection Questions

- How does knowing you are chosen change the way you approach God?
- What would staying close look like practically today?

Practice for Today

Write a note or reminder: 'I am chosen to stay close.' Place it somewhere you'll see it often today.

Prayer

Jesus, thank You for choosing me. Help me to treasure that invitation, and to remain near You with joy and confidence. Amen.

30

Peace Grows in the Shade

"Peace is not found in escape, but in deep-rooted presence."
— Thomas Merton

Scripture Meditation

"You will keep in perfect peace those whose minds are steadfast, because they trust in you." — Isaiah 26:3 (NIV)

Abiding is the slow planting of peace. When you dwell under the shelter of God's presence, peace begins to spread its shade over your anxious thoughts.

This peace is not the absence of problems—it's the presence of Christ. It grows as you rest, not as you strive. It steadies as you remain.

Let His peace cover you today like a canopy. Let it quiet the noise, still the storm, and ground your soul in sacred shade.

Personal Affirmation

I abide under the covering of peace. God's presence is my shelter and strength.

Reflection Questions

- What robs you of peace most often?
- How might abiding shift your response to stress or fear?

Practice for Today

Find a shady spot or create one in your mind. Breathe deeply and repeat: 'Your peace surrounds me.' Let that truth settle in.

Prayer

Prince of Peace, let me dwell in Your nearness. Let peace grow in the shade of Your love, and let it calm every anxious place in me. Amen.

31

The Ministry of Remaining

"Sometimes the greatest ministry is simply staying when others walk away." — Jean Vanier

Scripture Meditation

"Let us hold unswervingly to the hope we profess, for he who promised is faithful." — Hebrews 10:23 (NIV)

Abiding isn't just a private act of devotion. It becomes a ministry. When you remain—through pain, waiting, or unseen obedience— you bear silent witness to God's faithfulness.

Your endurance preaches. Your stillness reveals trust. Your refusal to disconnect becomes a living sermon to those around you.

Don't underestimate the ministry of remaining. Every moment you stay connected to the Vine, you offer the world a glimpse of the One who holds you fast.

Personal Affirmation

My quiet faithfulness is a testimony. My staying is a ministry.

Reflection Questions

- Where are you being called to simply remain right now?
- How can your faithfulness point others to Christ today?

Practice for Today

Think of someone watching your life. Pray: 'Lord, let my remaining inspire them to trust You more deeply.'

Prayer

Faithful God, use my life as a quiet sermon. Let my endurance reflect Your strength, and my stillness reflect Your presence. Amen.

32

Trusting the Invisible

"Much of God's work in us is hidden, but never wasted." —
Dallas Willard

Scripture Meditation

"So we fix our eyes not on what is seen, but on what is unseen." — 2
Corinthians 4:18 (NIV)

Abiding often feels unimpressive. There are no fireworks, no constant
spiritual highs. It is slow. Quiet. Hidden. And yet, it is in this invisible
space that God does His deepest work.

The world celebrates what can be measured. But the Kingdom values
what is unseen—faithfulness, trust, hidden obedience. Abiding is the
practice of trusting the invisible.

You may not always feel the growth. But if you are remaining, you are
being changed. God is never idle with a heart that abides.

Personal Affirmation

Even when I cannot see it, God is at work. I trust the invisible process
of grace.

Reflection Questions

- Where are you tempted to doubt God's work because you can't see results?
- How can you honour the hidden work of abiding in this season?

Practice for Today

Find something small and living—a leaf, a seed, a sprout. Let it remind you that growth often begins in secret places.

Prayer

God who sees in secret, help me trust You when I can't see the fruit. Let my hidden faith honour You, and bear eternal fruit. Amen.

33

Rooted Not Rushed

"Spiritual growth is not a sprint; it is a steady walk with the Savior." — Eugene Peterson

Scripture Meditation

"Let your roots grow down into him, and let your lives be built on him." — Colossians 2:7 (NLT)

The soul cannot grow in haste. Just like trees require time to grow roots deep into the soil, so your soul requires space, silence, and stillness to grow into Christ.

Abiding slows you down. It invites you to let go of spiritual urgency and embrace divine timing. The most beautiful fruit comes from the most deeply rooted lives.

Don't rush the process. Let God grow you deep, not just wide. What's rooted will remain, even when seasons shift.

Personal Affirmation

I am rooted in Christ, not rushed by life. My depth will determine my fruitfulness.

Reflection Questions

- Are you feeling hurried in your walk with God?
- What rhythms help you grow roots rather than chase results?

Practice for Today

Take five slow, deep breaths before each task today. Let them ground you in your identity as one who abides—not rushes.

Prayer

Lord, teach me to stay still long enough to grow deep. Root me in You, that I might bear lasting fruit. Amen.

34

From Striving to Resting

"The spiritual life is not about getting it right; it's about getting close." — Brennan Manning

Scripture Meditation

"In repentance and rest is your salvation, in quietness and trust is your strength." — Isaiah 30:15 (NIV)

We often think abiding means doing more, getting it right, proving ourselves faithful. But Jesus never invited us into striving—He welcomed us into rest.

Striving exhausts the soul. Resting restores it. To abide is to return to the posture of a child—trusting, leaning, present. The work has been finished. The invitation now is to remain.

Let yourself breathe. Let your soul rest in the truth that you are already loved. There is no need to perform when you've already been welcomed home.

Personal Affirmation

I am not striving—I am resting. God's love holds me, even when I let go.

Reflection Questions

- Where are you striving in your spiritual life?
- What does it look like to rest in God's love instead?

Practice for Today

Find a quiet place. Sit for ten minutes, repeating gently, 'I am loved. I am held. I can rest.'

Prayer

Jesus, I let go of striving. I choose to rest in Your love and let my soul be restored by Your presence. Teach me to abide with trust. Amen.

35

Obedience as Abiding

"Obedience is the fruit of love, not the price for it." — Elisabeth Elliot

Scripture Meditation

"If you keep my commands, you will remain in my love." — John 15:10 (NIV)

Abiding is not passive. It flows into obedience—not as duty, but as devotion. When you love someone deeply, you listen to their heart. You live to please them, not to earn their love, but because their love has already transformed you.

Obedience becomes a natural outflow of intimacy. It is not forced—it is formed in the place of connection. The more you remain, the more you desire to follow.

Let obedience be your offering today—an act of love, not fear.

Personal Affirmation

Obedience is my joy. I follow Jesus not to be loved, but because I already am.

Reflection Questions

- How do you currently view obedience—joyful response or heavy requirement?
- What command of Christ is speaking to your heart today?

Practice for Today

Ask God, 'What would loving obedience look like today?' Write down what comes and take one faithful step toward it.

Prayer

Jesus, I choose to obey—not to earn Your love, but because I already live in it. Let my obedience be an act of worship. Amen.

36

When You Feel Nothing

"Faithfulness is not always feeling; it is often choosing." — Teresa of Calcutta

Scripture Meditation

"We live by faith, not by sight." — 2 Corinthians 5:7 (NIV)

There are days when abiding feels effortless, and days when it feels like reaching for a God you cannot sense. But remaining with God isn't about always feeling—it's about always choosing.

The silence of your senses does not equal the absence of His Spirit. When you abide through numbness, doubt, or dryness, you offer a deeper faith—the faith that clings in the dark.

Even when you feel nothing, you are doing something holy: staying. And in the stillness, God is still moving.

Personal Affirmation

Even when I feel nothing, I choose to remain. My faith is rooted in God's presence, not my perception.

Reflection Questions

* What helps you stay close to God when your feelings fade?
* How might God be shaping your faith in the silence?

Practice for Today

Sit for five minutes in God's presence without expectation. Say: 'God, I choose You, even when I cannot feel You.'

Prayer

God of every moment—felt or unseen—I stay. I trust that You are with me, forming me in the quiet. Let my faith rise in the stillness. Amen.

37

Staying in Sacred Places

"The soul is healed by being with God more than by being busy for Him." — Richard Foster

Scripture Meditation

"Better is one day in your courts than a thousand elsewhere." — Psalm 84:10 (NIV)

Some places draw us deeper into God's presence—quiet rooms, sacred corners, sunlit benches, or early morning walks. These are more than locations; they are invitations.

Sacred places don't change God's nearness, but they help us notice Him. When you consistently meet Him in these places, your soul begins to anticipate Him there.

Make space for sacredness. Let the holy ground of quiet routine become the soil of deep connection.

Personal Affirmation

I make space to meet with God. Sacred places help anchor my soul.

Reflection Questions

- Where do you sense God's nearness most tangibly?
- How can you turn an ordinary place into sacred space today?

Practice for Today

Choose a consistent place to meet God. Sit there today with open hands and say, 'This is holy ground.'

Prayer

Lord, meet me in the ordinary and turn it into sacred. Let my still places become sanctuaries of Your presence. Amen.

38

Slow Fruit, Deep Joy

"Fruit that lasts is never fast. It ripens in hidden places of the soul." — John Mark Comer

Scripture Meditation

"The fruit of the Spirit is love, joy, peace, patience..." — Galatians 5:22 (NIV)

We live in a world of instant outcomes. But in the Kingdom, fruit is grown—not manufactured. It takes time, tenderness, and trust.

Abiding teaches us to be patient with the process. Joy doesn't erupt—it emerges. It flows from a heart consistently watered by grace, even through dry seasons.

Don't rush the fruit. Celebrate what is forming slowly. There is deep joy in becoming all God has planted you to be.

Personal Affirmation

I trust slow fruit and deep joy. God is growing good things in me.

Reflection Questions

- Where do you see signs of slow fruit in your life?
- What might joy look like as a fruit rather than a feeling?

Practice for Today

Take five minutes to give thanks for slow changes. Whisper: 'I trust the process. I welcome the fruit.'

Prayer

Lord of the harvest, grow joy in me. Even when I can't see it, let fruit form slowly, deeply, and beautifully through Your Spirit. Amen.

39

Remaining When It Hurts

"Sometimes abiding means trusting God when it aches, not just when it feels good." — Ruth Haley Barton

Scripture Meditation

"Though the fig tree does not bud and there are no grapes on the vines... yet I will rejoice in the Lord." — Habakkuk 3:17–18 (NIV)

Pain can tempt us to run. From God, from ourselves, from others. But abiding is the choice to stay, even when it hurts. Especially when it hurts.

Remaining in God's love during suffering is an act of trust. It says: 'You are still good. I will still be here.' This posture of pain becomes a testimony of profound faith.

God is not afraid of your ache. He remains with you in it—and gives you grace to do the same.

Personal Affirmation

I remain in God even through pain. His presence is my comfort and my strength.

Reflection Questions

- What pain tempts you to pull away from God?
- How have you seen God remain with you in past seasons of hurt?

Practice for Today

Light a candle or hold a cross. As you sit with your pain, whisper: 'Even here, I remain. Even now, You are near.'

Prayer

God of all comfort, I will not run. I remain. Meet me in this place of ache. Let my pain become soil for deeper trust. Amen.

40

The Gift of Being With

"The presence of God is not a concept to grasp but a companionship to enter." — Jean Vanier

Scripture Meditation

"Surely I am with you always, to the very end of the age." — Matthew 28:20 (NIV)

Abiding is not a task you accomplish. It is a relationship you nurture. God is not asking you to understand everything—He's asking you to be with Him.

There is profound grace in simply being with God. No performance. No perfect words. Just presence.

God's gift is not always a solution—it is Himself. And your gift to Him today is not your effort, but your company.

Personal Affirmation

I am with God, and He is with me. His presence is enough.

Reflection Questions

- What gets in the way of simply being with God?
- How can you grow in awareness of His presence throughout your day?

Practice for Today

Set a timer for five minutes. Sit in stillness. Don't say anything. Just be with God.

Prayer

Jesus, thank You for being with me. Teach me to treasure Your presence above everything else. Let my heart rest in the gift of being with You. Amen.

41

Secure in the Vine

"The vine does not abandon its branches—it supplies them." — Thomas à Kempis

Scripture Meditation

"No one will snatch them out of my hand." — John 10:28 (NIV)

In the chaos of life, you may question your connection. You may feel distant, disconnected, or doubting. But the truth is this: your security is not based on your grip on God, but His hold on you.

Abiding doesn't require perfection. It calls for trust in the Vine who never lets go. You may stumble, feel weary, or wander—but you are never outside His reach.

You are secure in the Vine. Held, sustained, and continually nourished by grace.

Personal Affirmation

I am held securely in Christ. Nothing can separate me from His love.

Reflection Questions

- Do you ever fear being disconnected from God?
- How does knowing you are secure in Christ bring peace?

Practice for Today

Clasp your hands tightly and say, 'Jesus, thank You for never letting go.' Let your hands remind you of His grip of grace.

Prayer

Faithful Vine, thank You that I am held in You. Even when I feel weak, You are strong. Keep me close, secure, and nourished in Your love. Amen.

42

The Still Work of the Spirit

"The Holy Spirit works most deeply in stillness, not in striving." — Catherine Doherty

Scripture Meditation

"Not by might nor by power, but by my Spirit," says the Lord Almighty. — Zechariah 4:6 (NIV)

So much of life is loud—noise, motion, hustle. But the work of the Holy Spirit is often quiet, still, and unseen. He moves like breath, soft but powerful.

Abiding trains you to lean into this gentle rhythm. The Spirit forms Christ in you through whispers, nudges, convictions, and comfort. The still work is the deep work.

Today, release the pressure to manufacture growth. Yield to the Spirit's quiet shaping. Trust that God does His finest work in silence.

Personal Affirmation

The Spirit of God is at work in me, even when I don't see it. I trust the stillness.

Reflection Questions

- How have you experienced the Spirit's work in quiet ways?
- Are you allowing room for the Spirit to move gently in your life?

Practice for Today

Spend five minutes in silence. Whisper, 'Holy Spirit, I welcome Your quiet work in me.' Then simply rest.

Prayer

Holy Spirit, thank You that Your power is made perfect in stillness. Quiet my soul to hear You. Form Christ in me gently and deeply. Amen.

43

Resting in His Nearness

"We search for God in the distance, while He is whispering from within." — Thomas Merton

Scripture Meditation

"The Lord is near to all who call on him, to all who call on him in truth." — Psalm 145:18 (NIV)

Abiding reminds you that you are never far from God. You don't have to reach across eternity to touch Him—He is already close, closer than your breath.

When life feels frantic or your prayers feel unheard, draw back into this nearness. You are not calling to a distant deity—you are leaning into the One who is already beside you.

Rest in His nearness. Let His closeness quiet your heart and become your calm.

Personal Affirmation

God is near. I rest in His presence and trust in His closeness.

Reflection Questions

* When do you forget that God is near?
* How can you intentionally return to that awareness today?

Practice for Today

Find a quiet moment. Place your hand on your chest. Whisper, 'You are near.' Let His presence surround you.

Prayer

Lord, You are closer than I think, nearer than I feel. Draw me into Your presence today, and let my soul find rest in Your nearness. Amen.

44

Rooted in Hope

"Hope is not wishful thinking. It's the anchor that keeps us abiding when everything shakes." — Corrie ten Boom

Scripture Meditation

"We have this hope as an anchor for the soul, firm and secure." — Hebrews 6:19 (NIV)

Abiding connects you to something stronger than emotion or outcome—it anchors you in hope. Not vague optimism, but living hope rooted in Christ.

This hope doesn't shift with circumstance. It doesn't crumble in waiting. It remains firm, because it is fixed on the unshakable faithfulness of God.

When you abide, hope becomes more than a feeling. It becomes your root system—deep, stable, and secure in the promises of God.

Personal Affirmation

My hope is rooted in Christ. I am anchored, not tossed. Secure, not shaken.

Reflection Questions

- What is currently challenging your sense of hope?
- How does abiding in Christ restore and strengthen your hope?

Practice for Today

Write down a promise from Scripture that gives you hope. Keep it visible and speak it over yourself throughout the day.

Prayer

God of hope, anchor me in Your Word and presence. Let my soul be steady, not because everything is perfect, but because You are faithful. Amen.

45

Letting Go to Remain

"We must be emptied of all that hinders so we may be filled with all that abides." — Meister Eckhart

Scripture Meditation

"Whoever loses their life for my sake will find it." — Matthew 10:39 (NIV)

Abiding sometimes requires subtraction. To remain in Christ, you may need to release what clutters, competes, or consumes.

Letting go is not loss—it is liberation. When your hands are no longer grasping other things, they are free to hold on to Jesus. Simplicity becomes sacred.

Abiding is not always about doing more. Sometimes it is about letting go—of fear, control, old identities, or lesser loves—so you can remain with your whole heart.

Personal Affirmation

I release what weighs me down. I remain in Christ with open hands and an undivided heart.

Reflection Questions

- What is God inviting you to let go of today?
- How might letting go help you remain more deeply?

Practice for Today

Take an object, like a stone or pen, and hold it tightly—then release it. Let it represent your willingness to let go and remain.

Prayer

Jesus, show me what to lay down so I may take hold of You. Help me release every weight that hinders my abiding. You are enough. Amen.

46

Remaining in the Ordinary

"The spiritual life is not elsewhere; it is here, in the dishes, the silence, the walking home." — Kathleen Norris

Scripture Meditation

"And whatever you do, whether in word or deed, do it all in the name of the Lord Jesus." — Colossians 3:17 (NIV)

Abiding is not reserved for mountaintop moments or morning devotions. It is lived in the mundane—in errands, emails, meals, and meetings.

Christ is present in the ordinary. When you learn to abide in the small things, you discover that no moment is secular. Every breath becomes sacred.

You don't have to escape life to remain in God. You simply invite Him into the middle of it. The Vine runs through every part of your day.

Personal Affirmation

God is in the ordinary. I abide in Him as I live, move, and breathe.

Reflection Questions

- Where have you separated the sacred from the ordinary?
- How might God be inviting you to abide in the midst of daily tasks?

Practice for Today

Pick one ordinary task—laundry, dishes, walking. Whisper a prayer during it. Let it become an altar of abiding.

Prayer

God of the everyday, help me see You in the small things. Let my life become a temple where even the ordinary becomes holy. Amen.

47

Worship That Remains

"True worship is abiding adoration—love sustained through all seasons." — Brother Lawrence

Scripture Meditation

"Worship the Lord in the splendour of his holiness; tremble before him, all the earth." — Psalm 96:9 (NIV)

Worship is not just a song—it's a way of staying. When you abide, your life becomes a steady melody of devotion, not just moments of praise.

Real worship lingers after the music ends. It is choosing to adore God when the lights are low, when the heart is heavy, when no one else sees.

Abiding worship is the fragrance of a life fully surrendered. It is a continual 'yes' to God, with every breath and step.

Personal Affirmation

My life is worship. I abide in adoration, not performance.

Reflection Questions

- How can your everyday actions reflect worship?
- What does it mean to worship through abiding rather than striving?

Practice for Today

Play a worship song. As you listen, whisper: 'This is my offering, Lord—not just the song, but my life.'

Prayer

Lord, let my whole life be worship. Let every moment of abiding be filled with Your beauty and Your presence. Amen.

48

When Remaining Feels Costly

"The cost of staying with Jesus is real—but so is the joy that follows." — Dietrich Bonhoeffer

Scripture Meditation

"Whoever wants to be my disciple must deny themselves and take up their cross daily and follow me." — Luke 9:23 (NIV)

Abiding sounds beautiful, but sometimes it hurts. Remaining means letting go of comfort, pride, control, and even approval. Jesus never hid the cost—He embraced it.

To remain in Him is to choose Him again and again, even when it's not convenient, popular, or easy. But there is a deep joy found in faithfulness. Joy that's forged in surrender and refined by grace.

If abiding feels costly, you're not doing it wrong. You're being shaped by love. The cross always precedes the resurrection.

Personal Affirmation

Even when it costs me, I choose Christ. He is worth every surrender.

Reflection Questions

- Where has abiding felt costly for you?
- How has God met you in those sacrifices?

Practice for Today

Identify one area of resistance. Offer it to Jesus in prayer. Whisper, 'I remain, even here. You are worth it.'

Prayer

Jesus, help me not to shy away from the cost of following You. Give me courage to remain when it's hard, and joy that surpasses the sacrifice. Amen.

49

Cling to the Vine

"To cling to Christ is to let go of every false vine." — Dallas Willard

Scripture Meditation

"Remain in me, as I also remain in you. No branch can bear fruit by itself." — John 15:4 (NIV)

There are many things we try to attach ourselves to—success, security, approval, even religion. But only one Vine brings life.

Clinging to the Vine means loosening your grip on everything else. It's not weakness—it's wisdom. The closer you hold to Christ, the freer your soul becomes.

Abiding is a daily act of reaching again for Jesus, even if your hands are trembling. He will hold you fast. He always has.

Personal Affirmation

I cling to Christ, the True Vine. His life flows through me and makes me whole.

Reflection Questions

- What false vines have you attached yourself to in the past?
- What helps you return and cling to Christ?

Practice for Today

Stretch out your arms like branches. Whisper, 'I cling to You, Jesus.' Let this physical act mirror your inner surrender.

Prayer

Jesus, You are the Vine. I am the branch. Help me to remain, to cling, and to trust in the life You alone give. Amen.

50

The Abiding Yes

"Each moment of surrender is a yes to divine love." — Henri Nouwen

Scripture Meditation

"For no matter how many promises God has made, they are 'Yes' in Christ." — 2 Corinthians 1:20 (NIV)

Abiding is not a one-time decision. It's a rhythm of daily yeses—yes to love, yes to presence, yes to surrender. Every yes, no matter how quiet, echoes in eternity.

There are days when your yes feels bold and confident, and days when it is whispered through tears. Both are sacred. Because your yes holds you in communion with the One who has already said yes to you.

Christ is the divine Yes to every longing. Abide in Him by saying yes again today.

Personal Affirmation

Today I say yes to God. In joy or weariness, my yes remains.

Reflection Questions

- What small yes is God inviting you to today?
- How does your yes shape your abiding journey?

Practice for Today

Write down the words: 'Yes, Lord.' Keep them visible today. Let them be your quiet offering of trust and love.

Prayer

God of the eternal Yes, thank You for always choosing me. Today, I choose You again. In weakness or strength, I say yes. Amen.

51

Remaining in Mystery

"God is not a puzzle to be solved, but a presence to be received." — Evelyn Underhill

Scripture Meditation

"Now we see only a reflection as in a mirror; then we shall see face to face." — 1 Corinthians 13:12 (NIV)

There will be things you do not understand—questions that remain unanswered, seasons that don't make sense. Yet the invitation still stands: remain.

Abiding is not about having all the answers. It's about staying in relationship even when you don't. Remaining in mystery means choosing trust over clarity, wonder over control.

God is not absent in the mystery—He is often most present there. Sometimes faith means standing in the fog and holding His hand anyway.

Personal Affirmation

I can remain in mystery because I trust the One who holds it all.

Reflection Questions

- What questions are you wrestling with today?
- How is God inviting you to abide in mystery rather than rush to certainty?

Practice for Today

Sit with one question you don't have the answer to. Instead of solving it, surrender it. Say, 'I trust You even here.'

Prayer

God of mystery and mercy, I choose to abide even in what I cannot see. Give me peace in the not-knowing and joy in the trusting. Amen.

52

Rooted in the Word

"Scripture is the soil where abiding faith takes root." — A. W. Tozer

Scripture Meditation

"If you remain in me and my words remain in you, ask whatever you wish, and it will be done for you." — John 15:7 (NIV)

To abide is to anchor yourself in the truth. God's Word is not merely to be read—it is to be absorbed, lived, and treasured.

When His Word remains in you, it transforms how you think, speak, and live. It becomes a lamp to your path and a mirror to your soul. The more deeply you are rooted in Scripture, the more fruitful your abiding becomes.

Don't skim the surface—sink your roots deep. Let the Word become your dwelling place.

Personal Affirmation

God's Word lives in me. I am rooted in truth and nourished by grace.

Reflection Questions

- What Scripture has recently stirred or anchored your heart?
- How can you remain more intentionally in the Word this week?

Practice for Today

Choose one verse. Write it down. Read it aloud. Meditate on it throughout your day. Let it dwell richly within you.

Prayer

Living Word, plant Your truth deep in me. Let my life reflect the beauty of Your promises and the power of Your presence. Amen.

53

When You Drift

"Abiding isn't about never drifting—it's about always returning." — Brennan Manning

Scripture Meditation

"Return to me, and I will return to you," says the Lord Almighty. — Malachi 3:7 (NIV)

Sometimes we drift. Not out of rebellion, but through busyness, distraction, or discouragement. The heart forgets its anchor. The soul wanders.

But the miracle of abiding is not that you never leave—it's that the door is always open. God welcomes you back, not with shame, but with embrace.

If you feel far off today, simply turn. The Vine hasn't moved. He's waiting—not with condemnation, but with love.

Personal Affirmation

When I drift, I return. I am always welcomed home by love.

Reflection Questions

- What signs tell you your heart is drifting?
- What helps you return quickly and gently to abiding?

Practice for Today

Pause and whisper: 'Lord, I return.' Sit in stillness, letting His grace surround you without shame.

Prayer

Faithful God, thank You for always welcoming me home. When I drift, draw me gently back. Let my heart rest again in You. Amen.

54

The Fruit of Remaining

"Fruit is not forced—it flows from the life of abiding." — Watchman Nee

Scripture Meditation

"This is to my Father's glory, that you bear much fruit, showing yourselves to be my disciples." — John 15:8 (NIV)

Abiding leads to fruit—not because you strive, but because you stay. Love, joy, peace, patience—these aren't goals to chase; they are evidence of a heart connected to the Source.

You don't force an apple tree to bear fruit—it happens because the roots are healthy. The same is true for your soul. The more you remain in Christ, the more naturally His character begins to grow in you.

Don't judge your journey by speed. Watch for signs of fruit—however small—and give thanks. You are growing.

Personal Affirmation

I am bearing fruit because I remain in Christ. His life flows through me.

Reflection Questions

- What fruit do you see emerging in your life as a result of abiding?
- How does staying connected to Christ help you reflect His character?

Practice for Today

Notice a moment today where love, joy, or patience flows from you. Pause and thank God—it is fruit of abiding.

Prayer

Lord, thank You that I don't have to strive to be fruitful—only stay. Let my life overflow with the beauty of Your Spirit at work in me. Amen.

55

Remaining Through Temptation

"Every temptation is an invitation—to either flee or remain." — C. S. Lewis

Scripture Meditation

"No temptation has overtaken you except what is common to mankind. And God is faithful..." — 1 Corinthians 10:13 (NIV)

Temptation isn't just about sin—it's about separation. It seeks to disconnect you from the Vine, to lure your heart away from intimacy.

To remain in Christ during temptation is not to be unaffected, but to be anchored. You may feel the pull, but you don't walk alone. The Spirit strengthens your yes to God and your no to everything less.

In moments of struggle, remember: you are not condemned. You are connected. You don't overcome by willpower, but by abiding.

Personal Affirmation

In temptation, I choose to remain. Christ is my strength and my victory.

Reflection Questions

- Where are you tempted to disconnect from Christ?
- How might remaining in Him reshape how you respond to temptation?

Practice for Today

In a moment of temptation, pause. Whisper: 'I remain in You, Jesus.' Let that be your anchor.

Prayer

Jesus, when I am tempted, help me remain. Let Your nearness be stronger than every lie and every lure. Amen.

56

Remaining in Community

"You cannot abide in Christ and disconnect from His body." — Dietrich Bonhoeffer

Scripture Meditation

"If we walk in the light, as he is in the light, we have fellowship with one another." — 1 John 1:7 (NIV)

Abiding is personal, but never private. The life of Christ flows through a body—not just a branch. To remain in Him is to remain connected to His people.

Community is messy and vulnerable. But it's also where grace becomes tangible, and where abiding faith is stirred and sustained.

You were not meant to remain alone. In the encouragement of others, you'll often hear the voice of Christ calling you deeper still.

Personal Affirmation

I remain in Christ and stay rooted in community. I grow stronger with others.

Reflection Questions

- How does community support your abiding?
- Where are you tempted to isolate rather than remain connected?

Practice for Today

Reach out to someone in your spiritual community. Share a word of encouragement or ask how you can pray for them.

Prayer

Lord, thank You for the gift of community. Help me stay connected, even when it's hard. Let our fellowship reflect the love of Christ. Amen.

57

The Beauty of Dependence

"True maturity in Christ is not independence, but deeper dependence." — John Stott

Scripture Meditation

"I am the vine; you are the branches. If you remain in me and I in you, you will bear much fruit; apart from me you can do nothing." — John 15:5 (NIV)

The world teaches us to grow up and become self-sufficient. But in the kingdom, spiritual maturity looks like deeper dependence.

Abiding is not about proving your strength—it's about admitting your need. To cling to Christ is to declare, 'I cannot do this without You.'

There is beauty in dependence, because it frees you from striving and anchors you in grace. The Vine does not expect you to sustain yourself. He simply asks you to remain.

Personal Affirmation

I am not ashamed of my need. My dependence on Christ is my greatest strength.

Reflection Questions

- Where do you feel tempted to rely on your own strength?
- What does it look like to lean more fully into Christ today?

Practice for Today

In prayer, say aloud, 'Jesus, I need You.' Sit quietly for a few minutes, letting that confession lead you deeper into rest.

Prayer

Lord, I confess my dependence. I cannot bear fruit without You. Be my source, my strength, and my stay. Amen.

58

Abide in the Waiting

"Waiting is not wasting when you are abiding in the One who holds time." — Ruth Haley Barton

Scripture Meditation

"The Lord is good to those who wait for him, to the soul who seeks him." — Lamentations 3:25 (ESV)

Waiting tests your roots. It stretches your trust. But it also deepens your abiding. In waiting, you discover the difference between outcomes and presence.

You may not have what you asked for yet, but you still have Him. And sometimes, the wait is what transforms you more than the arrival ever could.

Abiding doesn't make waiting easy—but it does make it sacred. Stay rooted. He is at work, even in the delay.

Personal Affirmation

Even in the waiting, I remain. My hope is anchored in God's goodness.

Reflection Questions

- What are you currently waiting on God for?
- How might He be shaping your heart in this season of waiting?

Practice for Today

Sit in silence for five minutes. As you wait, say, 'I trust You here, Lord.' Let your stillness become a sanctuary.

Prayer

God of the waiting places, meet me here. Grow patience in me. Remind me that You are not slow, but purposeful. Amen.

59

The Grace to Begin Again

"Abiding always begins with grace, not guilt." — Richard Foster

Scripture Meditation

"Because of the Lord's great love we are not consumed, for his compassions never fail. They are new every morning." — Lamentations 3:22–23 (NIV)

There will be days when you forget to remain—when distractions steal your focus, or weariness dulls your hunger. But grace always invites you back.

Abiding is not a performance. It is a rhythm of return. Every morning, every moment, you can begin again.

Don't wait to feel worthy. Don't let yesterday's failure disqualify today's connection. His mercies are new. His arms are open. Just begin again.

Personal Affirmation

I am not disqualified. God's grace welcomes me to begin again.

Reflection Questions

- Where do you feel the need for a fresh start in your spiritual life?
- How can you respond to God's mercy today?

Practice for Today

Take a deep breath. Speak these words: 'Lord, I begin again with You.' Let today be a reset, not a retreat.

Prayer

God of mercy, thank You for fresh starts. When I stray, call me back. When I forget, remind me. Let today be a new beginning in Your grace. Amen.

60

Remaining in the Storm

"Peace is not the absence of storms but the presence of Christ in them." — Thomas à Kempis

Scripture Meditation

"Then he got up and rebuked the winds and the waves, and it was completely calm." — Matthew 8:26 (NIV)

Storms reveal where you're rooted. When everything shakes, abiding anchors you in Someone who does not.

The presence of trouble is not the absence of God. In fact, He is often clearest in the storm—walking on waves, whispering peace, holding you fast.

Don't run from the storm. Remain in the presence of Christ, who never leaves, never fears, and never fails.

Personal Affirmation

Even in the storm, I remain in Christ. He is my peace and my anchor.

Reflection Questions

• What storm are you currently walking through?
• How might abiding in Christ change the way you navigate it?

Practice for Today

Take five deep breaths. As you exhale, say, 'Peace, be still.' Let Christ calm your soul even if the storm continues.

Prayer

Jesus, when the winds rise and the waves roar, let me stay with You. Be my calm in the chaos and my anchor in the unknown. Amen.

61

Resting Without Guilt

"Rest is holy. It is not a luxury, but a declaration of trust."
— Marva J. Dawn

Scripture Meditation

"Come to me, all you who are weary and burdened, and I will give you rest." — Matthew 11:28 (NIV)

Rest is an act of resistance in a world that glorifies hustle. It's not laziness—it's alignment. When you rest, you declare that your value isn't in what you produce, but in who you abide in.

Guilt often creeps in when we slow down. But Christ doesn't condemn your pause—He invites it. Abiding includes rest because relationship requires presence, not performance.

Let rest be worship. Let it renew your soul and remind you that you are deeply loved, even in stillness.

Personal Affirmation

Rest is not weakness. It is worship. I receive God's rest without guilt.

Reflection Questions

• Where do you feel pressure to earn your worth through activity?
• How might embracing rest deepen your abiding?

Practice for Today

Take a 10-minute break with no agenda. Breathe. Be still. Let it be enough.

Prayer

Jesus, teach me to rest without guilt. Help me receive Your invitation to abide, even in my pauses. Amen.

62

Fruitful in the Hidden Places

"Much of the soul's growth happens in the soil no one sees."
— Jeanne Guyon

Scripture Meditation

"Your Father, who sees what is done in secret, will reward you." —
Matthew 6:4 (NIV)

Abiding often looks unimpressive. It happens in the quiet corners, in
whispered prayers and faithful acts unseen by the crowd.

But the hidden places are not forgotten. God sees them. And it's in
those places that your roots deepen and your fruit quietly forms.

Don't underestimate the power of what happens when no one's
watching. The hidden places are where heaven often does its deepest
work.

Personal Affirmation

Even in the hidden places, I am growing. God sees me and delights
in my faithfulness.

Reflection Questions

• Where are you faithfully abiding without recognition?
• How does knowing God sees the hidden give you strength?

Practice for Today

Do one quiet act of love today—without telling anyone. Let it be an offering of hidden fruit.

Prayer

God who sees in secret, thank You for valuing what the world overlooks. Help me abide in the hidden places with joy and trust. Amen.

63

Remaining with a Tender Heart

"Spiritual strength is not hard-heartedness, but a heart softened by love." — Julian of Norwich

Scripture Meditation

"I will give you a new heart and put a new spirit in you; I will remove from you your heart of stone and give you a heart of flesh." — Ezekiel 36:26 (NIV)

Abiding in Christ will tenderize your soul. Over time, His love reshapes your responses—from defensiveness to gentleness, from self-protection to compassion.

The world teaches us to harden up, but Jesus invites us to remain soft—open to His voice, pliable to His touch, sensitive to His Spirit.

A tender heart is not weak. It's proof of a life deeply rooted in grace.

Personal Affirmation

I choose to remain tender. God's love is softening and shaping my heart.

Reflection Questions

- Where has your heart felt hardened lately?
- How is God inviting you to respond with tenderness today?

Practice for Today

Do one thing today that expresses tenderness—toward yourself, someone else, or God.

Prayer

Jesus, make my heart tender like Yours. Soften me where I've grown cold. Let Your love flow freely through every part of me. Amen.

64

The Stillness of Abiding

"It is in stillness that we most clearly hear the heartbeat of God." — Thomas Merton

Scripture Meditation

"Be still, and know that I am God." — Psalm 46:10 (NIV)

Stillness is not the absence of sound, but the presence of awareness. In a world that hurries, abiding invites you to pause and know.

You don't have to perform in stillness. You don't have to fix. You only have to be present—to let your heart rest against the rhythm of divine love.

The stillness of abiding reorients your soul. It silences fear, centers your mind, and awakens deep trust. In stillness, God is not distant—He is near.

Personal Affirmation

I make space for stillness. In quiet, I remember who God is—and who I am in Him.

Reflection Questions

- What keeps you from being still with God?
- How can stillness become a rhythm in your day-to-day life?

Practice for Today

Find five minutes to sit in stillness. No words. No requests. Just be present with the One who loves you.

Prayer

God of peace, still my soul. Teach me to pause, to listen, to abide. Let Your quiet presence restore me. Amen.

65

Abiding Through Transition

"God does not change—even when everything around you does." — Oswald Chambers

Scripture Meditation

"Jesus Christ is the same yesterday and today and forever." — Hebrews 13:8 (NIV)

Transitions can be unsettling. New seasons, shifting roles, or unexpected turns often leave us feeling untethered.

But the call to abide doesn't change with your circumstances. The Vine remains steady. Whether you're stepping into something new or letting go of something old, Jesus is the unchanging anchor.

In transition, you may feel uprooted. But spiritually, you are still deeply planted. Abide, even here. You are not alone in the unknown.

Personal Affirmation

Even in transition, I remain anchored in Christ. He is my constant and my guide.

Reflection Questions

- What transition are you currently navigating?
- How can abiding anchor you in this time of change?

Practice for Today

Name one change you are facing. Place your hand over your heart and say, 'Jesus, You remain.' Let it ground you in His presence.

Prayer

Lord, in every change, You are my unchanging peace. Help me abide in You through every unknown. Amen.

66

Abide Without Answers

"We live by faith, not by explanations." — Oswald Chambers

Scripture Meditation

"Trust in the Lord with all your heart and lean not on your own understanding." — Proverbs 3:5 (NIV)

There are seasons where the answers don't come. Prayers feel suspended. Logic fails. All you're left with is mystery.

Abiding doesn't always bring clarity. But it does bring presence. And sometimes presence is better than understanding.

When your questions echo in the silence, remember: Jesus is not absent. He's sitting with you in the unknown, offering Himself instead of an explanation.

Personal Affirmation

I do not need every answer. I abide in the One who holds them all.

Reflection Questions

- What unanswered question are you carrying today?
- How might abiding bring peace even without clarity?

Practice for Today

Write down your question. Fold it up. Place it before God as an offering of trust, saying, 'I trust You more than I need to know.'

Prayer

God of mystery, I surrender the need to understand. Let my faith rest not in explanations, but in Your unchanging presence. Amen.

67

When Abiding Looks Ordinary

"God walks among the pots and pans." — Teresa of Ávila

Scripture Meditation

"Whatever you do, work at it with all your heart, as working for the Lord." — Colossians 3:23 (NIV)

Abiding doesn't always feel sacred. Often, it looks like doing laundry, answering emails, or cooking dinner with grace in your heart.

The presence of God is not confined to cathedrals or quiet times. He is in the mundane, the repetitive, the unnoticed. When you invite Him into your ordinary, your ordinary becomes holy.

Abiding is not about escaping life's routine—it's about carrying God into it. Even the smallest task can become an altar.

Personal Affirmation

God is with me in the ordinary. Every moment matters when lived with Him.

Reflection Questions

- What daily task can become an invitation to abide?
- How can you practice God's presence in the midst of your routines?

Practice for Today

As you complete a simple task today, say aloud, 'This too is for You, Lord.' Let it become worship.

Prayer

Lord, teach me to find You in the ordinary. Let my daily life be a temple of Your presence. Amen.

68

Abiding in Weakness

"It is in our weakness that we become most aware of our need for abiding strength." — Amy Carmichael

Scripture Meditation

"But he said to me, 'My grace is sufficient for you, for my power is made perfect in weakness.'" — 2 Corinthians 12:9 (NIV)

Weakness is not failure—it's a doorway to deeper abiding. When you have nothing left to offer, you are finally ready to receive.

Abiding doesn't require strength. It only requires surrender. Christ meets you, not when you've got it all together, but when you come undone before Him.

Let your weakness lead you closer, not farther. In the place of limitation, His power is revealed most clearly.

Personal Affirmation

In my weakness, I abide. His strength sustains me.

Reflection Questions

- Where are you feeling weak or worn out today?
- How might that very place be a holy invitation to abide more deeply?

Practice for Today

Instead of hiding your weakness, name it in prayer. Whisper, 'Your grace is enough for me here.'

Prayer

Jesus, I bring You my weakness—not to be fixed, but to be held. Fill me with Your grace. Let Your power rest on me. Amen.

69

Remaining When It's Dry

"Spiritual dryness is not abandonment—it is often an invitation to deeper roots." — John of the Cross

Scripture Meditation

"Blessed is the one... whose delight is in the law of the Lord... That person is like a tree planted by streams of water." — Psalm 1:1–3 (NIV)

There will be seasons when your soul feels dry, when prayer feels empty, and Scripture seems distant. These are not signs of failure but invitations to go deeper.

In the dry times, the roots of your faith are tested. And often, they grow stronger. God may feel silent, but He is never absent. Sometimes He speaks loudest in stillness.

Remain, even when it feels like nothing is happening. Life is still flowing beneath the surface.

Personal Affirmation

Even in dryness, I remain. God is present and working underground.

Reflection Questions

- Have you experienced spiritual dryness recently?
- What does remaining look like when your soul feels empty?

Practice for Today

Write a short honest prayer. Even if it's just one line. Let your longing be your abiding.

Prayer

God of hidden waters, meet me in my dryness. Let my roots reach deeper. Teach me to remain, even here. Amen.

70

The Strength of Gentle Obedience

"Abiding love always expresses itself through surrendered obedience." — Elisabeth Elliot

Scripture Meditation

"If you keep my commands, you will remain in my love." — John 15:10 (NIV)

Obedience is not harsh—it's holy. It's the gentle strength that comes from trusting the One you love.

When you abide, obedience stops feeling like duty and starts flowing from desire. It's not about rules—it's about relationship. You obey not to earn love, but because you already have it.

Abiding teaches you that obedience is not a cage but a pathway to intimacy. Even the smallest yes becomes an act of worship.

Personal Affirmation

My obedience is not forced—it flows from love. I abide by saying yes to Him.

Reflection Questions

- In what area is God calling you to a gentle act of obedience?
- How does abiding help reframe the way you view obedience?

Practice for Today

Choose one small act of obedience today. Do it quietly, joyfully, as your abiding yes to God.

Prayer

Jesus, I love You. Let my love be expressed through joyful obedience. Teach me to trust You with every yes. Amen.

71

The Silence Between the Words

"God speaks most clearly in the silence between our thoughts." — Thomas Keating

Scripture Meditation

"In repentance and rest is your salvation, in quietness and trust is your strength." — Isaiah 30:15 (NIV)

Not every moment of abiding is filled with insight or activity. Sometimes, it's just sitting in holy silence—where no words are needed and nothing must be achieved.

There is a deep communion that happens in the quiet. Like a friend who needs no explanation, God waits in the space between your sentences. He is not in a rush. He delights in simply being with you.

Let the silence speak. It may say more than all your prayers combined.

Personal Affirmation

I am not afraid of silence. God is with me in the quiet, and that is enough.

Reflection Questions

- When was the last time you sat in silence with God?
- What fears or thoughts rise in you when there are no words?

Practice for Today

Sit in silence for five minutes. No asking. No fixing. Just be with God.

Prayer

God, I welcome the silence where Your voice grows louder. Let the stillness be sacred. Let me hear You in the hush. Amen.

72

Abiding When You Feel Nothing

"Faith is not a feeling—it's fidelity when feelings fade." —
Dallas Willard

Scripture Meditation

"For we live by faith, not by sight." — 2 Corinthians 5:7 (NIV)

There are days when your soul feels numb. The emotions have
quieted, and spiritual passion feels like a memory.

But abiding is not built on emotion—it's built on devotion. When you
remain in Christ through the dry, the dull, and the ordinary, you're
offering Him a deeper kind of love.

Feelings come and go, but faith abides. God sees every quiet act of
staying when nothing stirs your senses. And He is moved by your
unseen faithfulness.

Personal Affirmation

Even when I feel nothing, I remain. My faith is rooted in truth, not
emotion.

Reflection Questions

- Have you ever mistaken spiritual silence for absence?
- What helps you stay connected when your feelings waver?

Practice for Today

Read your favourite Scripture slowly. Let truth guide you, even when your heart feels distant.

Prayer

Lord, thank You that I don't have to feel You to remain in You. Anchor me in Your truth when emotions fade. I choose to stay. Amen.

73

Living from the Overflow

"The soul who abides will not just survive—they will overflow." — Andrew Murray

Scripture Meditation

"May the God of hope fill you with all joy and peace as you trust in him, so that you may overflow with hope." — Romans 15:13 (NIV)

When you remain in Christ, you're not just filled—you begin to overflow. Joy spills into discouragement. Peace quiets anxiety. Hope seeps into dry places.

Overflow doesn't come from striving. It's the result of staying. As you dwell in God's presence, His character begins to flow through your words, decisions, and presence.

You weren't made to run on empty. You were made to overflow with divine life.

Personal Affirmation

I abide in Christ, and my life overflows with His peace, joy, and hope.

Reflection Questions

- What areas of your life feel dry or depleted?
- How can you return to abiding so that you overflow again?

Practice for Today

Bless someone today out of your overflow—send encouragement, give generously, or pray quietly for them.

Prayer

Jesus, fill me again with Your life. Let my heart not just hold Your presence, but overflow with it. May others taste Your goodness through me. Amen.

74

When the World Moves Fast

"To abide is to slow your soul in a speeding world." — Ruth Haley Barton

Scripture Meditation

"Be completely humble and gentle; be patient, bearing with one another in love." — Ephesians 4:2 (NIV)

The world rarely slows down. Deadlines, demands, and distractions shout for your attention. But abiding whispers, 'Come away.'

Remaining in Christ isn't about removing yourself from the world, but about refusing to let its pace shape your soul. You move slower. Gentler. More rooted. More aware.

Even when the world rushes by, you can abide. You can walk through your day with a centered heart and an anchored presence. You are not of the storm. You are rooted in peace.

Personal Affirmation

The world may hurry, but I abide in peace. I move with God's unhurried rhythm.

Reflection Questions

- What parts of your life feel rushed or pressured?
- How can you slow down inwardly, even if life remains busy externally?

Practice for Today

Choose to walk slowly today at least once. With each step, whisper, 'You are with me, Jesus.'

Prayer

God of peace, teach me to live at Your pace. Let me walk with You, not run ahead. In every moment, help me remain. Amen.

75

The Courage to Stay

"Sometimes the boldest act of faith is simply staying." — Henri Nouwen

Scripture Meditation

"You did not choose me, but I chose you and appointed you so that you might go and bear fruit—fruit that will last." — John 15:16 (NIV)

There are moments when leaving feels easier—leaving the calling, the community, the quiet pursuit of God. But abiding is a form of courage. It is staying when it would be simpler to run.

Abiding faith does not always roar. Sometimes, it stands quietly in the midst of uncertainty and declares, 'I'm still here.' And that is enough.

When you feel tempted to walk away, remember that Christ first chose you. He remains with you, and by His grace, you can remain too.

Personal Affirmation

By grace, I stay. My courage is found in Christ who remains with me.

Reflection Questions

- Where do you feel tempted to give up or walk away?
- What might it mean for you to courageously abide today?

Practice for Today

Write down one place where you will choose to stay, to be faithful, even when it's hard. Offer that place to God.

Prayer

Jesus, give me courage to remain. When I am weary, hold me steady. Let my life be a quiet witness of faithful abiding. Amen.

76

Abiding in the Unknown

"God does not lead us by explanations but by His presence."
— Oswald Chambers

Scripture Meditation

"Your word is a lamp for my feet, a light on my path." — Psalm 119:105 (NIV)

The path ahead is not always clear. Sometimes you can only see the next small step—and even that feels uncertain. But abiding isn't about having a map; it's about staying close to the Guide.

When you remain in Christ, you walk in the light of His presence, even when the future is dim. You are not abandoned to guesswork—you are held, guided, and loved.

Abiding teaches you that you don't have to know everything. You just have to trust the One who does.

Personal Affirmation

Even in the unknown, I am held. I do not walk alone—I abide in the Light.

Reflection Questions

- What unknown are you currently facing?
- How is God inviting you to trust rather than strive for clarity?

Practice for Today

Take one step forward in something unclear today, whispering, 'Jesus, I trust You in the unknown.'

Prayer

God of mystery, I surrender what I do not understand. Lead me, one step at a time. I choose to abide, even here. Amen.

77

The Gentle Habit of Returning

"To return is the holiest rhythm of the abiding life." — Henri Nouwen

Scripture Meditation

"Return to the Lord your God, for he is gracious and compassionate, slow to anger and abounding in love." — Joel 2:13 (NIV)

The spiritual life is not a straight line. It's a circle of return. Again and again, we forget, we drift, we rush—and then we come home.

Abiding is not perfection. It is persistence. Every time you turn back to God—even with trembling, even with guilt—you declare, 'This is where I belong.'

And He always welcomes you. No lectures. No delay. Just love, waiting at the threshold, calling you back to rest.

Personal Affirmation

I return to God without shame. His mercy welcomes me again and again.

Reflection Questions

- Where in your heart do you need to return today?
- How can returning become a regular, gentle rhythm in your abiding life?

Practice for Today

Pause and say aloud, 'I return to You, Lord.' Let that be your breath prayer throughout the day.

Prayer

Gracious Father, thank You for always receiving me. Teach me to return quickly and often. Let my home always be in You. Amen.

78

The Joy of Being Known

"To be fully known and deeply loved is the essence of abiding in Christ." — Brennan Manning

Scripture Meditation

"Before I formed you in the womb I knew you, before you were born I set you apart." — Jeremiah 1:5 (NIV)

Abiding isn't just about knowing God—it's also about being known by Him. In His presence, there is no need to pretend, no mask to wear, no image to maintain.

You are fully seen and entirely loved. Even your weaknesses don't repel Him. In fact, they draw Him closer, because He delights to be your strength.

The joy of being known is the quiet foundation of all abiding. When you know you are loved as you are, you can stay, you can rest, and you can thrive.

Personal Affirmation

God knows me completely and loves me deeply. I am safe to abide in His presence.

Reflection Questions

- What parts of yourself do you find hardest to bring into God's presence?
- How might embracing His knowledge of you bring freedom?

Practice for Today

In prayer, say, 'You know me, Lord, and still You love me.' Sit with that truth in silence for a few minutes.

Prayer

Jesus, You know me—every part. Thank You for loving me without condition. Help me abide in that love and live from it. Amen.

79

Rooted in Unchanging Love

"God's love is not seasonal. It is the unshakable soil of your abiding." — A. W. Tozer

Scripture Meditation

"I have loved you with an everlasting love; I have drawn you with unfailing kindness." — Jeremiah 31:3 (NIV)

Many loves come and go. They flare with intensity and fade with time. But the love of Christ never shifts. It is steady, unwavering, and eternal.

When you abide, you root yourself in the only love that does not change. You stop trying to earn it. You start living from it.

God's love is not based on your performance—it's rooted in His nature. And when you truly believe that, your soul begins to rest.

Personal Affirmation

I am rooted in the unchanging love of Christ. I no longer strive—I remain.

Reflection Questions

*   Have you ever projected human inconsistency onto God's love?
*   What would change if you truly believed His love never changes?

Practice for Today

Write the words 'I am loved with an everlasting love' somewhere you'll see it today. Let it re-anchor your heart.

Prayer

Everlasting God, thank You that Your love never wavers. Root me deep in that truth. Let it nourish and transform me. Amen.

80

The Still Presence of Peace

"Peace is not the absence of trouble—it is the presence of Christ within it." — Brother Lawrence

Scripture Meditation

"And the peace of God, which transcends all understanding, will guard your hearts and your minds in Christ Jesus." — Philippians 4:7 (NIV)

True peace is not fragile. It doesn't depend on your circumstances but on your connection. Abiding in Christ allows His peace to govern your inner world, even when the outer one is chaotic.

This peace isn't passive—it's powerful. It guards your mind, calms your heart, and redirects your attention back to what's eternal.

Remain in Christ, and His peace remains in you. Still. Steady. Unmoved.

Personal Affirmation

I abide in the peace of Christ. His stillness surrounds and sustains me.

Reflection Questions

- Where do you need Christ's peace to reign today?
- How can you intentionally abide in that peace throughout your day?

Practice for Today

Breathe slowly for one minute. With each breath, say, 'Your peace remains.' Let it settle your spirit.

Prayer

Jesus, I receive Your peace. Not as the world gives, but as only You can give. Guard my heart as I abide in You. Amen.

81

Staying When the Fire Dies

"The test of love is not passion—it is perseverance." — Saint John of the Cross

Scripture Meditation

"Let us not become weary in doing good, for at the proper time we will reap a harvest if we do not give up." — Galatians 6:9 (NIV)

Spiritual passion ebbs and flows. The early fire may fade, replaced by steady embers. This isn't failure—it's formation.

Abiding love doesn't always feel fervent. Sometimes it's quiet faithfulness, showing up when the feelings don't. Staying when the spark seems gone.

Don't chase the flame—tend the fire. Your simple 'yes' in the ordinary is still devotion. God sees. God smiles. God stays.

Personal Affirmation

Even when the fire fades, I stay. My love is steady, and so is His.

Reflection Questions

- Have you confused emotional passion with spiritual depth?
- What does it mean for you to tend the fire of abiding love?

Practice for Today

Light a candle. As it burns, offer a simple prayer: 'Lord, keep me faithful, even when the flame is small.'

Prayer

Faithful God, teach me to remain when I feel nothing. Let my love grow roots deeper than emotion. I choose to abide in You. Amen.

82

The Comfort of His Nearness

"God is never far—He is nearer than your breath, nearer than your thoughts." — Madame Guyon

Scripture Meditation

"The Lord is close to the brokenhearted and saves those who are crushed in spirit." — Psalm 34:18 (NIV)

When life aches and your heart feels bruised, it's easy to wonder if God has stepped back. But the truth of abiding is this—He steps closer.

You are never alone in sorrow. His nearness is not always loud or dramatic. Sometimes, it's the quiet comfort that wraps around you without words.

Abiding is not about feeling brave. It's about staying close to the One who is your refuge. Even in the broken places, He remains.

Personal Affirmation

God is near. I am not alone in my pain—He abides with me.

Reflection Questions

* Where have you experienced the nearness of God in difficulty?
* How might His closeness be comforting you right now?

Practice for Today

Take a moment to place your hand over your heart and whisper, 'You are near, Lord.' Let His presence calm you.

Prayer

Jesus, thank You that You draw near to my broken places. Stay with me here. Let me rest in the comfort of Your nearness. Amen.

83

The Practice of Inner Stillness

"True abiding begins in a still heart, not in a silent room."
— Thomas Merton

Scripture Meditation

"In quietness and trust is your strength." — Isaiah 30:15 (NIV)

Stillness isn't just about shutting out the noise—it's about quieting the soul.

Abiding invites you to cultivate inner stillness, a posture of quiet trust that persists even amid chaos. This is where discernment grows, peace is anchored, and the voice of God becomes clearer.

Don't wait for perfect silence outside. Practice stillness within. You can be internally anchored even when the world is loud around you.

Personal Affirmation

I carry stillness in my soul. In Christ, I am calm, centered, and held.

Reflection Questions

- What disrupts your inner stillness most often?
- How can you return to that still place in God today?

Practice for Today

Find a quiet moment to close your eyes. Take slow breaths and repeat, 'You are my peace.' Let your soul settle.

Prayer

God of stillness, draw me inward today. Quiet my racing heart. Let Your presence anchor my soul in peace. Amen.

84

Bearing Fruit in the Background

"The fruit that lasts is often grown where no spotlight shines." — Dallas Willard

Scripture Meditation

"This is to my Father's glory, that you bear much fruit, showing yourselves to be my disciples." — John 15:8 (NIV)

You don't need to be seen to be fruitful. Some of the most powerful evidence of abiding—love, patience, forgiveness—grows in the unseen places.

Abiding fruit isn't always visible to crowds, but it's deeply valued by heaven. Your gentle word, quiet integrity, silent sacrifice—these are eternal seeds.

God is glorified not by how loud your life is, but by how deeply it is rooted in Him. Let fruitfulness flow from abiding, not striving.

Personal Affirmation

Even unseen, I am fruitful. God delights in the hidden growth of my abiding life.

Reflection Questions

- What 'hidden' fruit have you seen growing in your life?
- How might you celebrate fruitfulness without needing attention for it?

Practice for Today

Thank God for one area of quiet fruitfulness in your life today. Let it bring you joy.

Prayer

Father, thank You that nothing is wasted in Your kingdom. Help me stay rooted in You and trust You for the fruit, whether seen or unseen. Amen.

85

The Beauty of Consistency

"In the spiritual life, consistency is more powerful than intensity." — Eugene Peterson

Scripture Meditation:

"Let us hold unswervingly to the hope we profess, for he who promised is faithful." — Hebrews 10:23 (NIV)

A life of abiding isn't built on mountaintop moments—it's formed in the steady rhythm of showing up, day after day.

Spiritual growth rarely comes with fireworks. It looks like choosing prayer when you're tired, choosing love when you're wounded, choosing surrender when you don't understand.

Consistency isn't glamorous, but it is holy. It's the quiet heartbeat of a soul deeply anchored in Christ.

Personal Affirmation

In my consistency, I honour God. I am being formed, even in repetition.

Reflection Questions

- Where have you seen the fruit of spiritual consistency in your life?
- What area might God be inviting you to renew in faithful practice?

Practice for Today

Recommit to one small habit of abiding today—reading Scripture, praying, or simply pausing to breathe with God.

Prayer

Lord, thank You that faithfulness is more important than flashes of feeling. Make me steady, rooted, and consistent in Your love. Amen.

86

Abiding in the Waiting

"Waiting is not wasting when you are with the One who holds time." — Corrie ten Boom

Scripture Meditation:

"The Lord is good to those who wait for him, to the soul who seeks him." — Lamentations 3:25 (ESV)

Waiting is rarely comfortable. It stretches your patience, tests your trust, and reveals the desires buried deep.

But waiting is sacred when it becomes an invitation to abide. Instead of rushing ahead or grasping for answers, you choose to stay with God in the space between.

Abiding doesn't remove the wait—but it fills it with Presence. You are not just waiting for something—you are waiting with Someone.

Personal Affirmation

In the waiting, I am not alone. I abide with the One who is always on time.

Reflection Questions

- What are you currently waiting for in your life?
- How might you shift from waiting anxiously to waiting with God?

Practice for Today

Sit quietly for five minutes. Name your waiting. Then say aloud, 'I wait with You, Lord.'

Prayer

Faithful God, help me to abide even when answers delay. Teach me to trust that You are working while I wait. Amen.

87

Staying Through Disappointment

"Disappointment is the place where we learn to surrender again." — Elisabeth Elliot

Scripture Meditation

"The Lord is near to the brokenhearted and saves the crushed in spirit." — Psalm 34:18 (ESV)

Disappointment is heavy. It whispers lies about God's faithfulness and tempts you to pull away.

But the invitation of abiding is to stay—even in the sting. Even when things don't work out, when dreams crumble, or when people let you down, Christ remains.

Disappointment doesn't mean the end of hope. It means there's more to surrender. More to trust. And more grace to receive from the One who never walks away.

Personal Affirmation

Even in disappointment, I remain. Jesus stays with me, and His love does not fail.

Reflection Questions

- Where have you experienced disappointment recently?
- What might God be inviting you to surrender in that place?

Practice for Today

Write a short lament to God. Be honest. Then end it with one line of trust: 'Still, I choose to remain with You.'

Prayer

God of mercy, hold my heart in disappointment. Teach me to stay near, even when I don't understand. Let me find healing as I abide in You. Amen.

88

The Anchor of Abiding

"Abiding is the soul's anchor in the shifting seas of life." —
A. W. Tozer

Scripture Meditation

"We have this hope as an anchor for the soul, firm and secure." —
Hebrews 6:19 (NIV)

Life is uncertain. Circumstances shift. People change. Storms come.
But the soul that abides remains anchored.

Christ is your secure foundation—steadfast and unmoved. When
you dwell in Him, you're not tossed by every wave. You may feel the
wind, but you are not adrift.

Abiding is not escapism. It's the courage to remain stable, grounded,
and faithful in Christ, no matter what surrounds you.

Personal Affirmation

I am anchored in Christ. No storm can unroot me when I remain in
Him.

Reflection Questions

- What storm or pressure are you facing today?
- How can abiding in Christ become your anchor in this moment?

Practice for Today

Hold something small in your hand—a stone, a cross, a pendant—and whisper, 'Christ is my anchor.' Let the weight remind you of His stability.

Prayer

Jesus, be my anchor. Hold me steady when life shakes. Keep me rooted in You, unmoved by fear, and grounded in Your love. Amen.

89

A Steady Heart in a Shaking World

"The soul anchored in God need not fear the tremors of the world." — Teresa of Ávila

Scripture Meditation

"He will have no fear of bad news; his heart is steadfast, trusting in the Lord." — Psalm 112:7 (NIV)

News cycles shift, foundations shake, and fear can easily take root. But abiding in Christ trains your heart to remain steady, even when the world trembles.

It's not denial. It's confidence in a Kingdom that cannot be shaken. While chaos may surround you, your heart beats to the rhythm of heaven.

This is the gift of abiding—a heart that rests not in circumstance, but in the One who never changes.

Personal Affirmation

My heart is steady because I trust in the Lord. I will not be moved by fear.

Reflection Questions

- What external chaos has affected your internal peace?
- How can you strengthen your trust in God's unshakable presence?

Practice for Today

Read Psalm 112:7 aloud. Say it three times slowly. Let it root your heart in truth.

Prayer

God of peace, steady my heart. Let my spirit be anchored in You, not in headlines or uncertainty. I choose to abide in Your unshakable love. Amen.

90

The Abiding Life Is a Witness

"Abiding is not just for you—it's for the world watching you." — Dietrich Bonhoeffer

Scripture Meditation

"Let your light shine before others, that they may see your good deeds and glorify your Father in heaven." — Matthew 5:16 (NIV)

Abiding isn't only personal—it's also missional. A life that remains in Christ becomes a living invitation for others to do the same.

When people see peace in your storms, kindness in your weariness, or grace in your failure, they glimpse Jesus. You become a branch through which His life flows to others.

You don't have to strive to be a witness. You simply stay. The fruit of your abiding becomes the testimony of His love.

Personal Affirmation

As I abide in Christ, my life reflects His love. I am a witness without striving.

Reflection Questions

- Who in your life needs to see the fruit of Christ through you?
- How can your abiding life quietly point others to Him?

Practice for Today

Pray for someone who needs Jesus today. Ask God to use your life—without words if needed—as a gentle witness of His love.

Prayer

Jesus, let my life reflect You. As I abide, bear fruit through me that others may taste and see that You are good. Amen.

91

When Your Faith Feels Fragile

"God does not demand a strong faith—only a small one placed in a strong God." — Joni Eareckson Tada

Scripture Meditation

"A bruised reed he will not break, and a smoldering wick he will not snuff out." — Isaiah 42:3 (NIV)

There are days when faith doesn't roar—it barely whispers. Days when your belief feels threadbare and your prayers fragile.

But abiding doesn't require perfect faith. It only requires a willingness to stay. To lean in again. To hold on, even if by a thread.

God cherishes your fragile faith. He doesn't scold it—He shelters it. Abiding is not about the strength of your grip but the nearness of His hand.

Personal Affirmation

Even when my faith feels weak, I remain. God is holding on to me.

Reflection Questions

- What part of your faith feels fragile right now?
- How might God be meeting you gently in that space?

Practice for Today

Write a one-line prayer that honestly names your fragile faith. Offer it simply. Let it be enough.

Prayer

Tender God, I bring You my shaky belief. I don't have to be strong— just willing to stay. Thank You for holding me fast. Amen.

92

The Long Obedience of Love

"The spiritual life is not a sprint, but a long obedience in the same direction." — Eugene Peterson

Scripture Meditation

"Love never gives up, never loses faith, is always hopeful, and endures through every circumstance." — 1 Corinthians 13:7 (NLT)

Abiding is not a one-time decision—it's a lifelong direction. A posture of heart that keeps returning, trusting, loving, and following, day after day.

It's the love that wakes early to pray, stays soft in conflict, forgives when it hurts, and gives when it costs. This is the long obedience of love.

You may not see immediate fruit, but the roots are deepening. And in time, you'll find that abiding has changed everything—from the inside out.

Personal Affirmation

My love is rooted in Christ. I choose long obedience over quick emotion.

Reflection Questions

- What does long obedience look like in your current season?
- How is God strengthening your love through enduring faithfulness?

Practice for Today

Identify one long-term commitment—marriage, ministry, calling—and pray over it. Ask God for grace to abide through every season.

Prayer

Faithful God, help me to walk in long obedience. Teach me to love steadily, serve consistently, and abide deeply through every part of the journey. Amen.

93

Resting in His Faithfulness

"When we abide, we rest not in our strength, but in His unfailing faithfulness." — Charles Spurgeon

Scripture Meditation

"The one who calls you is faithful, and he will do it." — 1 Thessalonians 5:24 (NIV)

Your spiritual life doesn't rest on your ability to hold it all together. It rests on God's faithfulness.

Abiding invites you to stop striving and start resting. To trust that the One who called you will sustain you. He is faithful to complete what He started.

Let His consistency become your confidence. Even when you stumble, even when you feel weak—He remains faithful. That is where your rest begins.

Personal Affirmation

I rest in God's faithfulness. He will complete the good work He began in me.

Reflection Questions

- Where are you tempted to strive instead of trust?
- How can you rest more deeply in God's faithfulness today?

Practice for Today

Sit in silence for five minutes. As you breathe, repeat: 'You are faithful. I can rest.'

Prayer

Faithful Father, I lay down my striving. Teach me to trust in Your perfect faithfulness. I rest in You today. Amen.

94

The Reward of Remaining

"Abiding in Christ is not just the way to the reward—it is the reward." — Hudson Taylor

Scripture Meditation

"I am the vine; you are the branches. If you remain in me and I in you, you will bear much fruit." — John 15:5 (NIV)

The reward of abiding is not just peace, joy, or answered prayers. The reward is Christ Himself.

When you remain, you receive more of Him—His presence, His heart, His life flowing through yours. The longer you stay, the deeper you know Him. The more you dwell, the more you become like Him.

There is no greater reward than intimacy with Jesus. Every fruit of the Spirit, every grace-filled moment, every miracle of transformation flows from this one source—abiding in Him.

Personal Affirmation

Abiding in Jesus is my greatest joy and reward. In Him, I have everything I need.

Reflection Questions

- What have you come to treasure most in your abiding journey?
- How does Christ Himself satisfy your heart more than the gifts He gives?

Practice for Today

Spend five minutes in worship—no asking, just adoring. Let your heart rejoice in Jesus, the greatest gift of all.

Prayer

Jesus, You are my reward. More than blessings, more than answers—I want You. Keep me close. Keep me abiding. Amen.

95

Dwelling in the Heart of Christ

"To abide in Christ is to make your home in His heart." — Julian of Norwich

Scripture Meditation

"Whoever dwells in the shelter of the Most High will rest in the shadow of the Almighty." — Psalm 91:1 (NIV)

You are not just invited to believe in Christ—you are welcomed to dwell in Him. To settle your soul in His heart. To live, breathe, move, and rest in His love.

Abiding means you're not a guest or a visitor. You're home. You belong.

In Christ's heart, you find shelter in storms, healing for wounds, and joy that does not fade. This is where abiding leads—not to a distant God, but to a God who opens His heart and says, 'Stay.'

Personal Affirmation

I dwell in the heart of Christ. I am safe, loved, and fully at home.

Reflection Questions

- What does it mean to you to dwell in Christ's heart?
- How can you live more consciously aware of your home in Him today?

Practice for Today

Close your eyes and picture Christ's heart as your home. Rest there in silence for a few moments, receiving His love.

Prayer

Jesus, thank You for making a home for me in Your heart. Let me dwell there every moment of today—loved, known, and secure. Amen.

96

When Love Looks Like Staying

"Love is not always loud. Sometimes, it's the quiet courage to stay." — Amy Carmichael

Scripture Meditation

"Let us hold unswervingly to the hope we profess, for he who promised is faithful." — Hebrews 10:23 (NIV)

There are days when love doesn't feel emotional or exciting. It feels like faithfulness. Like showing up again. Like staying put when everything in you wants to escape.

Abiding is love that lingers. It's staying when you're misunderstood, remaining when you're unseen, and holding fast when hope feels distant.

God calls this love holy. And He Himself is the model—steadfast, unchanging, always present. When you stay, you reflect His very nature.

Personal Affirmation

My love remains. I abide with Christ, and He strengthens my heart to stay.

Reflection Questions

- Where is God calling you to love by staying?
- How does remaining in Christ empower your faithfulness?

Practice for Today

Write down one place in your life where staying is your act of love. Offer it as worship to God.

Prayer

Jesus, teach me to love by remaining. Strengthen me to stay rooted when I feel restless. Let my love reflect Yours—faithful, steady, enduring. Amen.

97

Letting the Word Dwell Deeply

"Let the Word of God sink deeply until it becomes the breath of your soul." — Dietrich Bonhoeffer

Scripture Meditation

"Let the word of Christ dwell in you richly." — Colossians 3:16 (ESV)

Abiding is not only about prayer or presence—it is also about the Word. The Scripture is not a task to complete; it is a place to dwell.

When the Word lives in you, it renews your thoughts, recalibrates your desires, and reminds you of truth when your emotions waver.

Let God's Word be more than a visitor. Make it your soul's permanent guest. Feed on it. Meditate on it. Let it shape your inner world.

Personal Affirmation

The Word of Christ dwells in me richly. It is my guide, my nourishment, and my delight.

Reflection Questions

- How does the Word currently dwell in your daily life?
- What Scripture has recently anchored or corrected you?

Practice for Today

Choose one verse from this devotion. Write it down and carry it with you today. Let it live in you.

Prayer

Lord, let Your Word live deeply in me. Make my heart its home. Let every thought, word, and action be shaped by Your truth. Amen.

98

Becoming Like the One You Dwell With

"We become like what we behold." — Gregory of Nyssa

Scripture Meditation

"And we all, who with unveiled faces contemplate the Lord's glory, are being transformed into his image." — 2 Corinthians 3:18 (NIV)

Abiding is not a passive posture—it is a transformational one. The more you dwell in Christ, the more you are shaped by His likeness.

This is not imitation—it is impartation. You don't become like Christ by copying Him, but by remaining in Him. His nature flows into yours like sap through a branch.

Every moment you behold Him in the Word, in worship, in silence— you are being changed. Slowly, steadily, beautifully.

Personal Affirmation

As I dwell in Christ, I am being transformed. His likeness is forming in me.

Reflection Questions

- Where have you seen yourself begin to reflect the heart of Christ?
- What area of your life needs more time abiding with Him to become like Him?

Practice for Today

Look in a mirror and say aloud, 'I am being made into the image of Christ.' Let that truth deepen your resolve to abide.

Prayer

Jesus, make me more like You. As I remain in Your presence, shape me, soften me, and make me reflect Your beauty. Amen.

99

Remaining in the Love That Remains

"There is no end to the love of Christ—only deeper places to dwell in it." — Catherine of Siena

Scripture Meditation

"As the Father has loved me, so have I loved you. Now remain in my love." — John 15:9 (NIV)

The final call of abiding is to remain in love. Not just feel it, but live in it. Build your home there. Trust it, receive it, and let it define you.

This love is not earned—it's given. It does not shift with your failures or fade in silence. It remains, always.

And when you remain in it, everything else begins to change. Fear loses its grip. Shame loses its voice. And love becomes not just what you receive—but what you give.

Personal Affirmation

I remain in the love of Christ. It surrounds me, shapes me, and sends me.

Reflection Questions

- How have you experienced the steady love of God in this season?
- What would it look like to remain in that love today?

Practice for Today

Place your hand over your heart and say, 'I am loved by God. I will remain in this love.' Let it be your foundation.

Prayer

Jesus, thank You for a love that never ends. Teach me to remain in it—secure, transformed, and fully alive. Amen.

100

Abide A Benediction

"To abide is to make your life one long yes to the love of God." — Thomas Merton

Scripture Meditation

"Now to him who is able to keep you from stumbling and to present you before his glorious presence without fault and with great joy." — Jude 1:24 (NIV)

This is not the end—it is the beginning. A deeper beginning. You have been invited into a life of remaining, not just visiting. A soul that stays, not just seeks.

Abiding is not a task to accomplish but a place to live. You will still wander, still forget, still drift—but now you know the way home.

Let your life echo with this quiet benediction: I will remain. In the Word, in the waiting, in the joy, in the sorrow, in the love that never lets me go—I will abide.

Personal Affirmation

I will abide. My life is rooted in the eternal presence of Christ.

Reflection Questions

- What has shifted in your heart through the journey of abiding?
- How will you continue this rhythm of staying with God beyond these pages?

Practice for Today

Write your own one-line benediction. A sentence that declares your intent to abide, even beyond this devotional.

Prayer

Jesus, I say yes again. To staying. To trusting. To loving You with all I am. Keep me in Your presence, and let my life be a long obedience of love. Amen.

Conclusion

A Life That Remains

This journey through abiding has not been about mastering disciplines or reaching spiritual milestones. It has been about coming home—to the Vine, to love, to presence.

You've taken one hundred steps deeper into intimacy, surrender, and transformation. But this is not the end. This is the invitation to a new way of being—with Christ, in Christ, and for Christ.

Abiding isn't a moment—it's a lifestyle. A continual return. A faithful remaining. As you step forward, carry the rhythms of stillness, Scripture, prayer, and presence with you. Let them mark your days and renew your nights.

When life becomes hurried, remember: the Vine never lets go. When you feel dry, return to the source. When you feel far, whisper His name. You are not called to strive, but to stay.

Jesus is still whispering: "Remain in Me, and I in you."

Reader's Benediction

May you remain in the love that never lets go.
May your roots grow deep in the soil of Christ.
May peace be your posture, and stillness your strength.
May your hidden life bear eternal fruit.
And may the God who called you to abide keep you abiding—day by
day, season by season, until you see Him face to face.

Amen.

Next Steps

1. Revisit the Journey
   Return to the devotions that spoke to your heart. Let them keep speaking.

2. Craft a Rhythm of Abiding
   Build a simple Rule of Life—a rhythm of prayer, Scripture, rest, and surrender.

3. Practice Sacred Pauses
   Set small reminders throughout your day to pause and reconnect with Christ.

4. Share the Invitation
   Invite others into the abiding life. Share this journey with your community, small group, or church.

5. Sow into Stillness
   Schedule regular moments of quiet with God—not as luxury, but necessity.

6. Live from the Vine
   Let love lead your actions. Let peace be your pace. Let His presence be your portion.

7. Stay Close
   Above all, stay near to Jesus. When everything else shifts, let His nearness be your anchor.

Closing Reflection: Living Abide

You've walked through a hundred days of intimacy with the Vine. But abiding doesn't stop with a devotional. It begins with a decision— daily, ordinary, holy—to remain.

A life that abides is not flashy, but faithful. Not rushed, but rooted. Not loud, but full of quiet strength. It is shaped by love, sustained by grace, and led by the Spirit.

Abiding is possible. Because Jesus remains in you.

Benediction

May you remain when the world pulls away.
May your soul stay rooted when the winds rise.
May your heart trust even in the silence.
And may your life speak of a love that never lets go.

You are called.
You are held.
You are chosen to abide.

Forever in the Vine.
Forever in Christ.

Bibliography

Amy Carmichael. *If.* Fort Washington, PA: CLC Publications, 1953.

Andrew Murray. *Abide in Christ.* London: James Nisbet & Co., 1882.

Brennan Manning. *The Ragamuffin Gospel.* Colorado Springs, CO: Multnomah Books, 1990.

Brother Lawrence. *The Practice of the Presence of God.* Whitaker House, 1692 (modern editions).

Catherine Doherty. Poustinia: Encountering God in Silence, Solitude and Prayer. Notre Dame, IN: Ave Maria Press, 1975.

Charles Spurgeon. *Morning and Evening.* London: Passmore and Alabaster, 1866.

Dallas Willard. *The Divine Conspiracy: Rediscovering Our Hidden Life in God.* San Francisco: HarperOne, 1998.

Dietrich Bonhoeffer. *The Cost of Discipleship.* New York: Macmillan, 1937.

Elisabeth Elliot. *Through Gates of Splendor.* Wheaton, IL: Tyndale House, 1957.

Eugene H. Peterson. *The Message: The Bible in Contemporary Language.* Colorado Springs, CO: NavPress, 2002.

Evelyn Underhill. *Mysticism: A Study in the Nature and Development of Spiritual Consciousness.* London: Methuen & Co., 1911.

Henri J.M. Nouwen. *The Return of the Prodigal Son: A Story of Homecoming.* New York: Image Books, 1992.

Hudson Taylor. *China's Spiritual Need and Claims.* London: Morgan & Scott, 1865.

Jean Vanier. *Community and Growth*. New York: Paulist Press, 1979.

Jeanne Guyon. A Short and Easy Method of Prayer. London: Thomas Baker, 1685.

John Mark Comer. *The Ruthless Elimination of Hurry*. Colorado Springs, CO: WaterBrook, 2019.

John Ortberg. *The Life You've Always Wanted: Spiritual Disciplines for Ordinary People*. Grand Rapids, MI: Zondervan, 1997.

John Stott. *Basic Christianity*. London: InterVarsity Press, 1958.

Joni Eareckson Tada. *Joni: An Unforgettable Story*. Grand Rapids, MI: Zondervan, 1976.

Kathleen Norris. *The Cloister Walk*. New York: Riverhead Books, 1996.

Meister Eckhart. *Selected Writings*. Translated and edited by Oliver Davies. New York: Penguin Classics, 1994.

Oswald Chambers. *My Utmost for His Highest*. Grand Rapids, MI: Discovery House, 1927.

Richard Foster. *Celebration of Discipline: The Path to Spiritual Growth*. San Francisco: Harper & Row, 1978.

Ruth Haley Barton. *Sacred Rhythms: Arranging Our Lives for Spiritual Transformation*. Downers Grove, IL: InterVarsity Press, 2006.

Thomas Keating. *Open Mind, Open Heart*. New York: Continuum, 1986.

Thomas Merton. *The Seven Storey Mountain*. New York: Harcourt, Brace and Company, 1948.

Watchman Nee. *The Normal Christian Life*. Fort Washington, PA: Christian Literature Crusade, 1957.

www.ingramcontent.com/pod-product-compliance
Lightning Source LLC
LaVergne TN
LVHW041153080426
835511LV00006B/581